2/7/11 FNR

Speak, Nabokov

# Speak, Nabokov

## MICHAEL MAAR

TRANSLATED BY
ROSS BENJAMIN

VERSO

London • New York

This edition first published by Verso 2009
© Verso 2009
Translation Ross Benjamin © 2009
First published as *Solus Rex. Die schöne böse Welt des Vladimir Nabokov*
© Berlin Verlag 2007

1 3 5 7 9 10 8 6 4 2

**Verso**
UK: 6 Meard Street, London W1F 0EG
US: 20 Jay Street, Suite 1010, Brooklyn, NY 11201
www.versobooks.com

Verso is the imprint of New Left Books

ISBN-13: 978-1-84467-437-4

**British Library Cataloguing in Publication Data**
A catalogue record for this book is available from the British Library

**Library of Congress Cataloging-in-Publication Data**
A catalog record for this book is available from the Library of Congress

Typeset by MJ Gavan, Truro, Cornwall
Printed in the US by Maple Vail

# Contents

# PREFACE

Nabokov's work is a forest in which it is easy to lose oneself and see nothing but the trees. Readers who penetrate somewhat deeper find themselves caught in a tangle of questions: Is there a hidden allusion to Shakespeare's *King Lear* when Humbert Humbert takes poor Lolita in his "marb*le a*rms"? What is the significance of Professor Pnin's final address at 999 Todd Road? Is it true that Nabokov deliberately places a key sentence about his uncle as though with tweezers on page 243 of his autobiography, *Speak, Memory*?

Nabokov trains his interpreters to be cabbalists. They quickly notice that simple questions do not have simple answers. In his work, it is precisely the simplest questions that are the most knotty. To begin with: Who actually wrote the books? We don't know whether it was the writer Sebastian Knight who invented his biographer-brother or vice versa. To this day we don't know who is supposed to have written *Pale Fire*, the poet or the commentator—or are they secretly identical, like Dr. Jekyll and Mr. Hyde? On these questions, interpreters are divided. Seven experts, eight opinions—because the best of them can change their minds. Among Nabokovians, little is certain and scholars rarely agree. There is one question, though, that they leave untouched: What difference would it make if, in the attic of a Swiss hotel or in an archive in New York, a literary testament were found in which Nabokov had provided solutions to all the riddles and answered all the questions? Wouldn't every word still be the same?

The enigmatic character of a work does not by itself preserve it from fading. The charms of the surface are no less important than those of the depths. In the construction of his involuted universe Nabokov is unsurpassed, but what makes him a great writer is something else. Other authors can be profound, but few have his casual wealth of details and tricks. It is this richness that makes him unique and yields the rewards of rereading. In Nabokov's work the old always appears as new, an effect that is quite rare and difficult to achieve.

Nabokov is fully present everywhere in his work; even the tiniest sliver contains the whole. And that is why each of these slivers scintillates with a dazzling spectrum of colors—a magic that is hard to convey in analysis. Wherever we open one of his books, we find him in his entirety. On every page there is one metaphor, one astonishing twist that could have come only from him. And now and then the reader stumbles on simple truths spoken as asides, which could seem sentimental were they not embedded as hard little stones in glittering sand and diamond dust. One sometimes has the impression that all the glitter perhaps serves only to conceal these small, hard truths. Nabokov puts such a lapidary sentence into the mouth of Pnin, who has to teach himself not to think of the death of Mira, the love of his youth, in Buchenwald, because "no conscience, and hence no consciousness, could be expected to subsist in a world where such things as Mira's death were possible." This sentence, which could be effective only in its aesthetic embeddedness, has been smuggled in by Nabokov the moralist; Nabokov the jeweler holds his protective hand over it.

For the cabbalists, such sentences fall through the sieve. These scholars are partial, perhaps somewhat too much so, to Nabokov the riddler and the sphinx.[1] The following study will not share this reluctance to take into account the person whose soul and imagination are crystallized in the art. The trees, their bark, and the bugs crawling beneath them shall not escape its attention—but above all it will not lose sight of the whole dark forest.

---

1   A notable exception is Michael Wood's extraordinarily insightful 1994 study *The Magician's Doubts: Nabokov and the Risks of Fiction.*

# 1

# THE MEDUSA EXPERIENCE

He had actually wanted to write about the love life of Siamese twins, but his wife forbade it.[1] The subject of the book that was rejected by five American publishers before the Paris-based Olympia Press—which otherwise brought out titles such as *The Sexual Life of Robinson Crusoe*[2]—took pity on it was not much more sensible, however. In December 1955 Graham Greene was the first to recommend the two light green volumes to the public as noteworthy literature, but it was less the endorsement than the reaction to it that generated excitement. The conservative

---

1  This anecdote comes from Nabokov's first biographer, Andrew Field. In 1951 Nabokov announced to a group of his colleagues: "I am now going to write about the love life of Siamese twins," whereupon Véra immediately interrupted, "No you're not!" Thus, *Lolita* would be, as Field quips, the "retreat into positively reasonable subject matter." (Andrew Field, *VN: The Life and Art of Vladimir Nabokov*, 287.) But ultimately Lolita's creator never completely gave up on the tale of the Siamese twins. Reduced to a short story, it finally appeared in 1958 as "The Double Monster." Field, who had won and then broken the trust of the master, becoming the viper in his bosom that soured his old age (and indirectly inspired the distorted biography of the late novel *Look at the Harlequins!*)—Nabokov's sloppy first biographer, the black sheep of the scholarly community—is worth a few words precisely because of this general ostracism. Paradoxically, Nabokov almost comes off better in this first biography than in the work of his second and much more rigorous biographer, Brian Boyd. Why? Because Boyd is fair and benevolent, whereas Field is full of resentment. Nabokov, who nonetheless appears so likable, has thus gone through all the trials by fire and water. With Boyd one doesn't know for sure what he, gentleman that he is, might omit out of consideration for his subject; with Field one suspects he would use even the tiniest, most fragile thread to try to hang Nabokov. But especially regarding Nabokov's foibles, Field in fact has a sharp eye—and overall, his book remains worth reading despite its unreliability.
2  To be sure, the Olympia Press also published Henry Miller and Jean Genet.

columnist John Gordon responded to Greene by declaring the work the filthiest book he had ever read—"sheer, unrestrained pornography."[3] The novel's triumph could no longer be stopped. *Lolita* became a *succès de scandale.*

Nabokov owed his mainstream breakthrough to a misunderstanding. The audience had not been expecting great literature but titillation. This misjudgment enabled Nabokov to take leave of his career as a lecturer and withdraw into the Grand Hotel in Montreux as a permanent guest. There he lived with his wife and his books in splendid isolation, translated *Lolita* into Russian, and produced his strange late work. Confronted in a 1969 interview with Tolstoy's statement that life was a *tartine de merde*, which one was obliged to eat slowly, Nabokov was amused. "The old boy was sometimes rather disgusting," he remarked. His own life was "fresh bread with country butter and Alpine honey."[4]

And yet it was not all a picnic. Ultimately, he remained a stranger everywhere, ever since he had been banished from the parks of his St. Petersburg childhood. Whether in Cambridge or in Berlin, on the American East Coast or Lake Geneva, the exiled writer was nowhere truly at home. When he fled Paris for New York with his wife and son in 1940 in the face of the advancing German army, he took little with him other than his mental library and his as yet obscure work: a number of stories and nine Russian novels. He was an impoverished, jobless émigré, one of the many writers without an audience. He was not an exiled prince mingling with the common folk, yet that was precisely the impression he made. A minor reputation had followed him like a faithful puppy from Europe, where the Russian émigré community regarded him as a prophet: If he could play chess only half as well as he could write, they said, he could spot Alekhine a pawn.[5] With the help and support of Edmund Wilson he

---

3   Boyd, *Vladimir Nabokov: The American Years*, 295.
4   Nabokov, *Strong Opinions*, 152.
5   Boyd, *The Russian Years*, 479. Further evidence of this reputation: Fondaminsky informs Nabokov that the very mention of the latter's name sends the great Bunin into a fit. "Of course he doesn't like you. You spread it all around that you're the best Russian writer." Nabokov responds, "What do you mean I spread it around?" "Well, you write," Fondaminsky sputters. (Stacy Schiff, *Véra: Mrs. Vladimir Nabokov*, 83.)

gradually became known in America, too. And finally came the work that —after an auto-da-fé thwarted by his wife (in a dispirited moment he had nearly incinerated the manuscript)—he successfully completed in December 1953. "*Lolita* is having an unbelievable success," he wrote to his sister five years later, as the book vied with *Doctor Zhivago* for number one on the bestseller lists. "But all this ought to have happened thirty years ago."[6]

That sounds more resigned than one would expect from an author who almost never showed a sign of despondency in public. With Nabokov it's hard to forget his public image—even more so than with other authors. More effectively than anyone else, he managed to establish a particular persona. The official Nabokov knows no regret and is brimming with self-confidence. When he sends a publisher a copy of *Lolita*, he writes, "A number of words are not in Webster, but will be in its later editions."[7] And he makes this remark *before* fame knocks at his door.[8]

The official Nabokov is that of his meticulously prepared interviews, which he collected in *Strong Opinions*. They show a man alone on a cliff, surrounded by a sea of mediocrity. "Jolly good view from up here" is his reply when asked in 1971 about his position in the world of letters.[9] From that height he delivered famous verdicts—brief, biting execrations of false idols and overrated dwarves such as Dostoyevsky, Stendhal, Balzac, T. S. Eliot, and Thomas Mann. Only a few got away in one piece. But those whom he loved, he loved truly. A mandarin, uncompromising and proud, he was not a man to tangle with, as his friend Wilson soon found out.

---

6   *Selected Letters*, 259.

7   Ibid., 251. It seems to be an almost physiological reaction among major but not yet recognized authors to produce the vitamin of praise themselves before they become emaciated by the scurvy caused by its deficiency. At some point they announce how brilliant their work is.

8   That *Lolita* was on the verge of becoming a bestseller did not yet amount to fame. Fame would come when a letter addressed to "Vladimir Nabokov, New Orleans"— one of the few American cities where Nabokov had never been—reached its addressee in Montreux. (See Schiff, *Véra*, 272.) It is the same fame that ensured that a letter addressed to "Hans Andersen, Denmark," found its way across the Atlantic to its recipient.

9   *Strong Opinions*, 181.

This image, which Nabokov constructed with the help of his wife, Véra, prevails to this day.[10] It can be expressed in a word: mastery. The author, even if he might have occasionally erred, was always in command and above the fray. It is easy to give examples that contradict this reputation. To take just one from his time as a professor at Cornell: Professor McConkey, who took over Nabokov's European Novel course after the latter's departure, recalls how his predecessor once stormed out of the classroom into the office in such a state of agitation that McConkey feared the poor man was about to have a stroke. Stammering, his face flushed, Nabokov told him what was wrong. A student had asked whether he himself could say something about Dostoyevsky, since Nabokov refused to put the author on the syllabus. It was impertinent, McConkey heard Nabokov shouting when he reached the chairman's office—the boy should be expelled from the university![11]

---

10   How decisively Véra contributed to the construction of this persona has been demonstrated by Stacy Schiff in her biography of Mrs. Vladimir Nabokov. Edmund Wilson in particular testified to Véra's strict regime: she "disapproved" when Wilson brought a magnum of champagne, "disapproved" when he gave Nabokov a copy of *Histoire d'O*, and frowned on all the little sins of her husband, whom she, according to Wilson, had under her thumb.

11   At Cornell, the Dostoyevsky despiser was known for being sensitive. He could take even the most harmless remark the wrong way. The same McConkey relates how Nabokov reacted when he told him he had read *Pnin* and liked it very much. He asked, "Why?" McConkey answered truthfully: because of the compassion he found in it. Nabokov "abruptly turned away, as if I had slapped his face." Nabokov's Russian colleague Marc Szeftel also had ambivalent experiences with him. That he had to serve as a prototype for Professor Pnin, who despite his endearing core was outwardly very much a caricature, was hard enough to swallow, but the author of *Lolita* could also be prickly in close collaboration. During his first year at Cornell, Nabokov wanted to teach a course on *The Song of Igor's Campaign*, but found the English translation unsatisfactory. Szeftel and Roman Jakobson, the prominent head of Harvard's Slavic Department, had been working for years on a commentary to the twelfth-century Russian epic. The three agreed to collaborate on a new English edition of *La Geste du Prince Igor*. Jakobson convinced the publisher to offer Nabokov as translator double the fee that he and Szeftel would receive for providing the comprehensive commentary. Nabokov did not manage to submit his translation by the May 1954 deadline, but at a meeting with Szeftel, he readily accepted corrections proposed by his colleague, who had penetrated more deeply into the material. Three years passed, and then Nabokov officially terminated his collaboration in a harsh letter to Jakobson: "After a careful

Nabokov's mastery was certainly no façade; it was more like a bamboo house, which leans in a storm and then rights itself. That furtive sigh about the belated success of *Lolita* reveals a more vulnerable man than the mandarin. Perhaps Nabokov was actually the shy, withdrawn man he once, in a rare moment, professed to be, who strove to conceal his vulnerability from his enemies and admirers alike.[12]

In any case, the true Nabokov is to be found in his work, in which his inner self radiates in all directions. That Nabokov, who reveals himself— realizes himself, in the strict sense of the word—in his art, is a different Nabokov from the shaman who holds his contemporary world and posterity under his spell. And it is this inner Nabokov who is crucial for us here.

---

examination of my conscience, I have come to the conclusion that I cannot collaborate with you. ... Frankly, I am unable to stomach your little trips to totalitarian countries, even if these trips are prompted merely by scientific consideration." Jakobson's last scholarly trip to Moscow, to which the letter alluded, had been a year earlier, and the fact that Nabokov's reaction to it came so late might have had less to do with the author's scrupulous examination of his conscience than something that had happened a few weeks earlier, about which the letter remains conspicuously silent. For years, Nabokov had inquired of Jakobson about the prospect of a job for him at Harvard. In the spring of 1957 this moment seemed to have arrived. There was a vacancy in the Slavic Department, but Jakobson instead preferred a scholar with a Ph.D. To the objection that Nabokov was a great Russian author, he replied: "Gentlemen, even if one allows that he is an important writer, are we next to invite an elephant to be professor of zoology?" Nothing became of the Harvard professorship, and from that point on Nabokov was hostile toward his former collaborator. Not only did he henceforth refer to Jakobson as a Bolshevik agent, he also began to view *The Song of Igor's Campaign* in a different light. Jakobson had made its authenticity into an article of faith. Was it not actually a forgery from a later century? Nabokov began to look for arguments for this doubt, which had evidently never troubled him before. In 1960, six years after the scheduled deadline, he finally published his translation of *The Song of Igor's Campaign* without commentary and with a different publisher. Neither Szeftel nor Jakobson is even mentioned in it. Szeftel, overlooked once again, commented bitterly in his diary: "Great talent does not necessarily make for great people." (See Diment, *Pniniad*, 24–41 and notes.)

12  See *Eigensinnige Ansichten, Gesammelte Werke* XXI, 120.

## The Horror Behind the Shimmer

This focus doesn't make matters easier, for that inner self is not solid like a block of marble. On the contrary, Nabokov describes with striking regularity a fundamental experience of fluidity.

One manifestation of this state is akin to the feeling that overcomes Goethe's young Werther: time and again the young Nabokov seeks images for a sense of all-embracing sympathy that ecstatically overflows the boundaries of the self. In the early story "Gods," the narrator senses in his blood the "rotation of unexplorable universes."[13] The 1935 story "Torpid Smoke" depicts the sensation as one of being permeated: the self feels like a medusa through which throbs of water pass.[14] The medusa experience is one of harmony with the universe and pantheistic bliss. It is the moment on a summer day when the fragrance of carnations, June rain, and the sounds of Bach from a piano merge into a mysterious unity:

> It was as if my soul had extended countless sensitive feelers, and I lived within everything, perceiving simultaneously Niagara Falls thundering far beyond the ocean and the long golden drops rustling and pattering in the lane. I glanced at a birch tree's shiny bark and suddenly felt that, in place of arms, I possessed inclined branches covered with little wet leaves and, instead of legs, a thousand slender roots, twining into the earth, imbibing it. I wanted to transfuse myself thus into all of nature, to experience what it was like to be an old boletus mushroom with its spongy yellow underside, or a dragonfly, or the solar sphere. I felt so happy that I suddenly burst out laughing ...[15]

Werther has a similar experience of nature. His pantheistically attuned soul is capable of ecstasies that are not available to every love-struck man. But this type of soul is also in greater danger than the solid, self-contained soul of Lotte's husband. All-embracing sympathy can change suddenly into its opposite, as Werther's suicide shows. The sense of dissolution can also be interpreted more coldly and clinically: as typical of the narcissist's permeable ego boundaries.

---

13 See *The Stories of Vladimir Nabokov*, 46.
14 Ibid., 397.
15 Ibid., 15–16.

The young Goethe and the young Nabokov, two captivating figures in the world of literature, both depicted the medusa experience at its two extremes. One pole is the bliss when the veil of Maya falls and the self recognizes its oneness with birch tree, mushroom, and dragonfly. But when that veil falls, something else can be revealed.

In 1926 Nabokov wrote the story "Terror." In a note he alludes to its autobiographical character: like a child who can't help glancing at the place where he has hidden something, he explicitly assures the reader that the story was written in one of the happiest years of his life.[16] The fact that there is virtually no contrivance to the story already lends it an autobiograpical flavor. There is no glitter and magic; the bag of tricks remains closed; there is scarcely any plot. The reason the story has been written is provided in the opening sentence: "Here is what sometimes happened to me …" The terror wants to articulate itself; it seeks words for the state in which the Medusa shows her Gorgon head.

The narrator, a poet, receives a foretaste of the terror when he comes out of a nocturnal work trance, turns on the light in his bedroom, and suddenly no longer recognizes himself in the mirror. He cannot reconcile the face looking back at him with the concept "I." He's had similar episodes before: a feeling of mortal dread erupting in bed at night, and the terror that once seized him in his lover's room at the mere fact of her presence. But these feelings are only small particles of the supreme terror that he proceeds to describe.[17] He goes away on a trip and sleeps badly for three nights and not at all on the fourth (like his author he has terrible insomnia). On the fifth day comes the part of his story that he wishes could be set in italics. When he steps into the street, he suddenly sees the world "as it really *is*." His mind refuses to accept the houses, trees, and people as "houses," "trees," and "people." What follows, the outbreak of terror, is the flipside of the celebrated feeling of all-embracing sympathy:

> My line of communication with the world snapped, I was on my own and the world was on *its* own, and *that* world was devoid of sense. I saw the

16   Ibid., 648.
17   Ibid., 174.

actual essence of things. I looked at houses and they had lost their usual meaning—that is, all that we think when looking at a house: a certain architectural style, the sort of rooms inside, ugly house, comfortable house —all this had evaporated, leaving nothing but an absurd shell, the same way an absurd sound is left after one has repeated sufficiently long the commonest word without heeding its meaning. ... I understood the horror of a human face. Anatomy, sexual distinctions, the notion of "legs," "arms," "clothes"—all that was abolished, and there remained in front of me a mere *something*—not even a creature, for that too is a human concept, but merely *something* moving past.[18]

Here the world no longer reveals its divine essence. The connection between self and world has been severed. Words become absurd husks, concepts dissolve. In his fictional Lord Chandos letter, published in 1902, Hugo von Hofmannsthal—of whom Nabokov had a surprisingly high opinion[19]—sounded similar themes and coined the famous image of words that disintegrate in the mouth like rotten mushrooms. A quarter of a century later Nabokov transformed his experience of the loss of language and world into fiction. "Terror," his Chandos letter, is a key to the horror behind the shimmer—the other pole of the medusa experience.

The ecstatic pole never vanishes completely: as late as in his autobiography, Nabokov describes the bright side of the experience as "a sense of oneness with sun and stone."[20] The implosion of this feeling—its pure, pitch-black negative—is illustrated in "Terror." In the end, however, the plot takes an unexpected turn. After his breakdown, the narrator learns via telegram that his lover is dying. She had just been in fine health—the poorly motivated twist exhibits the arbitrariness of the fiction, a mere mock-up behind which a disturbing experience seeks expression. The apparently paradoxical consequence is that the narrator's terror abates.

---

18    Ibid., 177. (Italics in original.) That the first-person narrator is resting on a bench in a public park when the world suddenly opens under him anticipates a key scene in *Pnin*.

19    See the interview with Dieter E. Zimmer (1966) in *Eigensinnige Ansichten*, 576.

20    *Speak, Memory*, 139.

Instead of increasing, the terror disappears. The death of his beloved saves him from insanity.

Fear of insanity already anticipates the psychic states of Nabokov's characters in his later novels. Many of them exist on the brink of madness. Charles Kinbote in *Pale Fire* lives in a parallel world in which regicides are hunting him. Hugh Person in *Transparent Things* has nocturnal, somnambulistic episodes to which his wife falls victim. Vadim Vadimovich in *Look at the Harlequins!* fears for his mental health because, though he can otherwise function, he finds himself incapable of a simple mental maneuver: visualizing himself turning on his heel so that right becomes left and vice versa.

Nabokov once called the writing of fiction a "rare variety of madness."[21] Throughout the oeuvre that owes its existence to this rare illness, the medusa experience throbs from beginning to end—with a systolic–diastolic fluctuation between horror and shimmer.

·

---

21   *Stories*, 405.

# 2

# MAGICIAN AND DWARF

And yet the illness wasn't really all that rare. What Hofmannsthal described in the Chandos letter touched a nerve at a time when neurasthenia was in fashion. Many writers were acquainted with the alternation between narcissistic dissolution and horror, between feelings of omnipotence and those of annihilation. One German author in particular suffered from this affliction. His narcissism was revealed to posterity through his posthumously published diaries. "I am also suffering both physically and psychically from the fact," one reads there more with amusement than pity, "that all No. 4 underwear is now too small for me, No. 5 too big.— Acid stomach and constipation."[1] That was the diaries' tone, and the sufferer was the great Thomas Mann.

The medusa experience cannot have been unknown to him. It was linked to the sense of outsiderness. His work—which ultimately drove him, like Nabokov, into exile in America—is populated by such outsiders. Adrian Leverkühn, his late Doctor Faustus, exemplifies the type as much as the early Tonio Kröger. At the head of this famous procession stands the title character of a story Mann published in 1897: "Little Herr Friedemann." From that point on, Mann later remarked, he had found the "discreet forms and masks" through which he could communicate his experiences.[2] It was a quite simple camouflage technique with which the author processed in his fiction the belated but intense awakening of his sexuality. As an outsider *in sexualibus* he transposed a psychological

---

1    Mann, *Diaries, 1918–1939*, 123. Entry of November 20, 1921.
2    Mann, *Death in Venice and Other Stories*, xv.

deviation into a physical defect.[3] The "little Herr" with the "Mann" in his name was a cripple.

What does all this have to do with Nabokov? After fleeing from the Revolution, he initially studied Russian and French literature at Cambridge, but mainly wrote poems, played tennis, tended goal in soccer, and had a number of affairs. In 1922 he moved from Cambridge to Berlin, not because he was particularly keen on being among the Germans, but rather because his family lived there—his mother, to be precise—and because the huge Russian community enabled him to exist in an intimate circle and to avoid as much as possible the natives of the host country.

Nabokov later made this avoidance of all things German into a point of honor. Despite the fifteen years he would ultimately spend in Berlin, he claimed never to have mastered the German language. How he was none-theless capable of translating Heine and Goethe into Russian, correcting the German translations of his work, or reading Freud in the original would be a mystery if we weren't dealing here with one of the legends that Nabokov circulated from time to time. The legend of his abstinence from German emerged after the Second World War. At the height of the war, he had compared the Germans to hyenas that it would be best to chloroform.[4] It's obvious that he no longer wanted to have—or ever to have had—anything to do with these hyenas. And it's equally obvious that a linguistic genius like Nabokov could scarcely live in a country for fifteen years without absorbing at least some of its language by osmosis. After all, how could he declare that Sigmund Freud should be read in the original German if he hadn't mastered a fair amount of the language?

Already in the twenties, he had not been fond of the Germans (or, to be exact, the Berliners—a very particular type). That didn't prevent him from studying their art and literature. In the course of his life, Nabokov became more conversant than many a Germanist with German Classicism

3 This technique was not uncommon. Herman Bang had already likened homosexu-ality to a deformity. (See "Gedanken zum Sexualitätsproblem," in *Forum Homo-sexualität und Literatur* 10 [1990], with an introduction by Heinrich Detering, 63–81.)
4 See *Selected Letters*, 47.

and Romanticism.[5] He was also more familiar with contemporary German literature than he later admitted. He knew enough German to read Bruno Frank or to be influenced by a novella titled *Lolita*, by Heinz von Lichberg.[6] And those were minor authors compared to the writer who had achieved fame with *Buddenbrooks* and whose next great, acclaimed novel, *The Magic Mountain*, found a very attentive reader in Nabokov. It wasn't long before the X-ray image of a lung on the seductress's night table and an aristocratic head nurse slowly and provocatively shaking a thermometer turned up in Nabokov's fiction too.[7]

*The Magic Mountain* appeared in 1924. The same year, Nabokov published his story "The Potato Elf," which remains among his lesser-known works. It is, one discovers with surprise, a response to the story of the cripple with which Mann made his breakthrough.

### Friedemann and the Potato Elf

"It was the nurse's fault."[8] With one of his striking opening sentences Thomas Mann begins the story of Johann Friedemann, who leads a solitary life due to his deformity. The carefully balanced existence with which the

---

5  Nabokov's knowledge of German Classicism and Romanticism is apparent not only in the notes to his Pushkin translation, but also in *Lolita*. See also 36, n. 35.

6  See Maar, *The Two Lolitas*. The old debate about Nabokov's German proficiency was reignited after the discovery of this 1917 novella by the journalist Lichberg, who later celebrated Hitler's rise to power and wrote for the *Völkischer Beobachter*. More than one Nabokovian was eager to downplay the German proficiency of the one true *Lolita* author as much as possible. It was in a television interview in 1975 with Bernard Pivot that Nabokov, deviating from the script, made his remark that one should read Freud in the original. (See *Eigensinnige Ansichten*, 172.)

7  Not Adriatica von Mylendonk, but Amalia von Wytwyl. (See *Bend Sinister*, 159, 224.) Not long after the publication of *The Magic Mountain*, Nabokov alluded to the novel in the 1927 story "An Affair of Honor": "Strange things kept happening: the book he was holding, a novel by some German writer or other, was called *The Magic Mountain*, and 'mountain,' in German is *Berg* …" (*Stories*, 211.) Of all books it is this one, which depicts a duel ending in death, that falls into the protagonist's hands shortly before a dreaded duel. Later Sebastian Knight will write a book titled *The Funny Mountain*. Further evidence and examples of Nabokov's fixation on the *Magic Mountain* author follow in the text.

8  Mann, *Death in Venice*, 3.

hunchback has made himself reasonably content collapses when Friedemann encounters the wife of the new district commandant, Gerda von Rinnlingen. She becomes his fate and his goddess of death. Friedemann cannot escape her demonic gaze. The consolations with which he had previously deceived himself now seem vapid to him. His weak resistance cannot stand up to the eruption of the elemental. When Gerda takes him aside and asks him with apparent sympathy about his affliction, it all comes pouring out of him. He confesses to her the misery of his life, and when she spurns him with a scornful laugh, he drowns himself in the river.

The end that Nabokov dreams up for his diminutive protagonist is somewhat less dramatic, but not only is there a remarkable similarity in tone; there are also startling parallels in the details. It was the nurse's fault ... why exactly was that? Because she was an alcoholic and dropped the baby on the floor, which led to his deformity. Nabokov, too, begins his story with an explanation of what made the eponymous protagonist a cripple: His father "drank like an old whale."[9] In his intoxication, he puts a wax dummy into the bed of his pregnant wife, and her shock causes the child's stunted growth. Like Friedemann, the Potato Elf remains a little man—to be precise, a dwarf—as a result of external harm. His name is Fred (not Fried, to be sure), he is in the circus, and on the first page is compared with the famous Swiss dwarf Zimmermann.[10] Zimmermann never comes up again; he is a mere name, transparent enough for anyone who wishes to see this or that Mann showing through.

Fred and Friedemann grow up chastely and are male old maids by the time they encounter their first and last femme fatale—Gerda in Friedemann's case, a woman named Nora in Fred's. Both manage to wrest a quiet, surrogate happiness from their lonely lives. Friedemann plays violin; Fred reads three or four novels per week and plays his pianola. But these consolations don't prevent the virginal dwarf from being beset now and then by "sharp pangs of lone amorous anguish."[11] And it's no different for little Herr Friedemann:

---

9  *Stories*, 228.
10  Ibid.
11  Ibid., 230.

One summer afternoon when he was taking a solitary walk along the promenade outside the old city wall, he heard whispered words being exchanged behind a jasmine bush. He cautiously peeped through the branches, and there on a seat sat this [shyly admired] girl and a tall red-haired boy whom he knew very well by sight; the boy's arm was round her and he was pressing a kiss on her lips, which with much giggling she reciprocated. When Johannes had seen this he turned on his heel and walked softly away.

His head had sunk lower than ever before between his shoulders, his hands were trembling and a sharp, biting pain rose from his chest and seemed to choke him. But he swallowed it down, and resolutely drew himself up as straight as he could. "Very well," he said to himself, "that is over. I will never again concern myself with such things. To the others they mean joy and happiness, but to me they can only bring grief and suffering. I am done with it all. It is finished for me. Never again."[12]

The main difference in Nabokov's story? Instead of embracing behind a jasmine bush, the couple does so behind brambles:

As the years passed, the yearning for a woman's love sighed in him fainter and fainter ... True, there were certain times, certain vague spring evenings, when the dwarf, having shyly put on short pants and the blond wig, left the house to plunge into crepuscular dimness, and there, stealing along some path in the fields, would suddenly stop as he looked with anguish at a dim pair of lovers locked in each other's arms near a hedge, under the protection of brambles in blossom. Presently that too passed, and he ceased seeing the world altogether.[13]

Fred's and Friedemann's peaceful lives are destroyed by the eruption of eros. The women with whom they fall in love are marked by a conspicuous lack of femininity. Gerda von Rinnlingen is a smoking, horseback-riding, mannish woman; her eyes, her laugh, and her movements "are simply not at all calculated to appeal to men."[14] Fred falls in love with a smoking, bony woman, who, like Gerda, is childless and somewhat masculine; in her final appearance she even has a mustache.[15] But the little

12  Mann, *Death in Venice*, 6–7.
13  *Stories*, 242.
14  Mann, *Death in Venice*, 11.
15  See *Stories*, 244.

men cannot resist the woman's gaze. "She had forced him to look away! She had humbled him with her gaze! Was she not a woman and he a man? And had not her strange brown eyes positively quivered with pleasure as she had done so?" The gender roles waver in this somewhat sado-masochistic encounter, after which a "voluptuous hatred" wells up in Friedemann.[16] Nora, too, keeps staring at Fred "with odd intensity" during their final encounter; she, too, does not take her "glistening eyes" from the dwarf. The goddesses of death play with the stigma of the deformed. They lure them out of their reserve and listen to them with apparent compassion, meanwhile thinking only of their own troubles. The confession that pours out of Friedemann doesn't do him any good; Gerda drives him to suicide with her laugh. Nora sleeps with Fred only to take revenge on her perpetually absent husband, the conjuror Shock. Gerda's mocking laugh has its echo in Nora's postcoital scorn for Fred, whom she thinks of as a "nasty little worm."[17]

The end that Nabokov has in store for Fred is sweeter than that of little Herr Friedemann. Fred dies too, but he dies a happy death. Nabokov's plot is markedly more refined than Mann's straightforward, linear development. After his brief affair with Nora, who goes on tour with her husband in America, Fred retreats to a town in the north of England. After eight years, Nora pays him a surprise visit and tells him that she had a son by him. Fred misses the past tense, fails to notice that she's dressed all in black, and misconstrues her sobs. At the sight of his happiness she refrains from explaining. With a gaping crowd in his wake, the dwarf runs to the train station to visit his son, and—having been sick already for a long time —dies of a heart attack in blissful anticipation.

Nabokov's story abounds with subtle mirrorings. Before Nora betrays her husband with the dwarf, she imagines Fred is her son. The implied incest motif reverberates softly eight years later, when Nora scrutinizes the dwarf's features eagerly and sadly for traces of resemblance to the son who has just died.[18] Even the final misunderstanding is foreshadowed early on.

---

16  Mann, *Death in Venice*, 18.
17  *Stories*, 244, 238.
18  Ibid., 244.

15

A deception is perpetrated by Shock, whom Nabokov depicts as a poet in disguise—*his* alter ego is unmistakably this magician rather than the dwarf. Shock lives entirely for his art and appears to be constantly distracted, but is secretly pulling all the strings. The dwarf and Shock are friends. Out of pity, Fred would rather conceal his misdeed from the conjuror. Nonetheless, out of consideration for Nora, whom he thinks he will thus be sparing a painful confession, he chivalrously brings himself to tell Shock the truth at a restaurant. But due to Shock's notorious absentmindedness, Fred's words fall on deaf ears. Shock returns home to his wife, who, in the wake of her infidelity, is "quivering with evil glee." When he pours some liquid from a vial into his glass of wine, she is not yet suspicious; even when he tells her that he has drunk poison and she shouldn't have been unfaithful to him (he had understood Fred's confession all too well), she takes it for one of his usual tricks. Only when her husband writhes in spasms and collapses on the bed with clenched teeth does she run to the telephone. When she returns in tears, the conjuror is standing "in white waistcoat and impeccably pressed black trousers" before the mirror. Adjusting his bow tie, he gives Nora "an absentminded twinkle."[19]

It is not only in the refinements of the plot that Nabokov shows in "The Potato Elf" how the theme of "Little Herr Friedemann" can be better approached. His motifs are subtler, he has more tricks, and his psychology is richer. And he sees more—the green pompom on Mrs. Shock's slipper, from which Fred cannot detach his gaze as she runs her fingers through his hair, or a miniature window shining on the side of a cup, which Johann Friedemann presumably would not have noticed. Even if the circus theme brings Nabokov closer to his weaker side—the sphere of the sad clown and the glittering top hat from which white doves soar[20]—his dwarf is aesthetically on a par with little Herr Friedemann.

---

19   Ibid., 238, 240.

20   This weaker side of Nabokov was also noted by the great American short story writer John Cheever: "I open Nabokov and am charmed by this spectrum of ambiguities, this marvelous atmosphere of untruth ... but his imagery—the shadow of a magician against a shimmery curtain, and all those sugared violets—is not mine." (*The Journals of John Cheever*, 184.) A perfume of violets; that's not far off the mark. Nabokov

We can take leave of the Potato Elf by noting the key motifs that already converge in this early story: the artist as egomaniac; the outsider whose sorrows never cease; the demonic, somewhat masculine woman; a whiff of misogyny; precise knowledge and outdoing of the competition.

It was good for Thomas Mann's well-being that he was never aware of Nabokov's disdain. Though Mann admired the Russian writer Merezhkovsky, who was acquainted with Nabokov and in 1935 gave a lecture titled *With Jesus or Sirin?*,[21] the German writer did not suspect that he was under the sharp scrutiny of this Sirin, pseudonym of the young Nabokov. And this was not the charitable Sirin, but the Sirin who scourged the moneychangers from the temple.

Nabokov's contempt for Thomas Mann ran deep: How could anyone name that quack in one breath with Proust and Joyce? Only the "fraud and fake" Eliot was worse than he—"and with more brains." *Death in Venice* was "asinine." "The Railway Accident" began with the grace of an elephant. Mann's shoddy work rested on a swamp of clichés. The characters existed only to represent general ideas. The prose was "plodding" and "garrulous," the psychology "artificial," and the humor reminded him of *Max and Moritz*.[22]

---

has a slight, unfortunate penchant for the circus metaphor, for clowns and tightrope acts, magicians and gypsy girls; a slight air of Leoncavallo that sometimes leads him to the brink of kitsch. Elsewhere in his minor works, he occasionally ends up at this brink. To give an example: in *Solus Rex* a comely little peasant girl is abducted for an hour from her parents' village by the lascivious crown prince Adulf. When she returns to the village, she is holding in one hand a hundred-crown note and in the other a fledgling that had fallen out of its nest. (See *Stories*, 538.) More than a few *poshlost* feathers cling to this little bird—to use the scathing Russian term for all that is exquisitely kitschy with which Nabokov loved to excoriate his foes.

21   See Field, *Life and Art*, 197.

22   This chain of invectives taken in succession: for Thomas Mann as a "quack," see *Dear Bunny, Dear Volodya: The Nabokov-Wilson Letters*, 164; for "fraud and fake," see ibid., 263; for *Death in Venice* as "asinine," see *Strong Opinions*, 57; for "grace of an elephant," see *Eigensinnige Ansichten*, 445ff.; for "nothing but clichés," "plodding and garrulous," "remindful of that of Max & Moritz," see *Selected Letters*, 525–26. In the case of "The Railway Accident," incidentally, Nabokov manages not even to mention the point of the story (a writer believes his manuscript has been destroyed and decides to begin again from scratch). In his polemical furor, Nabokov occasionally lost sight of

That wasn't meant as a compliment—and it did injustice not only to the author of the Joseph novel, but also to Wilhelm Busch, a genius akin to Gogol. Was Nabokov the widow Bolte, whose chickens Max and Moritz fish out of her pot? That is to say: Was there perhaps a note of jealousy in his attacks on the Nobel laureate and plaster idol? The mandarin was human, after all, with the emotional spectrum of other human beings. Resentment toward the Stockholm committee that honored so many unworthies instead of him is occasionally detectible in his interviews.[23] That might also play a role with respect to Mann, but something else is decisive here: the way Nabokov's scorn stimulates the poetic plasma of his work. It is there, in the stories and novels, not in the letters and interviews, that his iconoclasm takes a truly astonishing form.

## Mermaids and Hetaerae

Like Fred and Friedemann, the two authors are more connected than they seem at first glance. Long-cherished animosity implies commonalities. The Eskimo doesn't matter to the Indian; the Pakistani does. The most brutal wars are civil and fratricidal ones. Along with Freud and Dostoyevsky, Mann occupies a few posts in the borderland that Nabokov claims for himself alone.

An important arena in this disputed territory is the fairy tale. Little Herr Friedemann falls in love with a fairy-tale woman. It's no accident that Gerda von Rinnlingen takes her first name from the main character in Hans Christian Andersen's "The Snow Queen." Friedemann can no more escape from this queen with the strangely flickering eyes than can Andersen's Kay, who follows her into her Arctic ice palace. Gerda and

---

the admirable English golden rule for every fight: to attack one's opponent where he's strong, to meet him at his own level.

23  "In Russia lives the quite gifted poet Pasternak," began a Sirin review from 1927, when it was not yet foreseeable that decades later the gifted poet would oust a tender nymphet from the top of the bestseller lists with a thick novel and, even more unforgivably, would become the first Russian since Bunin to receive the Nobel Prize. His reward was inclusion on Nabokov's list of his favorite hate objects, the "four doctors": "Dr. Freud, Dr. Zhivago, Dr. Schweitzer, and Dr. Castro." (*Strong Opinions*, 115.)

Kay, the fairy-tale children under the spell of the Snow Queen, roam through Mann's world from the start.[24] But Nabokov, too, was under the spell of the Danish writer.[25] His work, too, is much more fairy-tale-like than it outwardly reveals. And the Snow Queen appears in it in various guises. The famous beginning of the fairy tale even plays a hidden key role in his novel *Pnin*.

Andersen's story begins with a splinter falling into little Kay's eye. This splinter is a tiny piece of the devil's shattered mirror, and it turns Kay into a rather arrogant and boastful boy. In *Pnin* Nabokov sets the first encounter between the narrator, Vladimir, and his main character, Pnin, in the waiting room of a doctor—to be precise, an ophthalmologist. It is not a splinter that has entered little Vladimir's eye, but a speck of coal dust. Is it any wonder that he turns out to be rather boastful and arrogant in the course of the novel? In case the reader's memory needs a little refreshing, Nabokov even weaves in the creator of the devil's mirror by name. Pnin's surrogate son displays artistic talents, which prompt his parents to wonder whether he inherited them from a great grandfather named Hans Andersen. The parenthetical caveat, "no relation to the bedside-Dane," also draws the cursory reader's attention to this very relation.

In the same sentence follows the most glittering piece of malice that Nabokov dreamed up with respect to Mann. Hans Andersen had been— take note!—a stained-glass artist in Lübeck before losing his mind and believing himself to be a cathedral.[26] The man from Lübeck with the excessive self-importance fuses with the fairy-tale Dane into one person. The sideswipe is not only comical in its indemonstrability—wide, inno- cent eyes after accomplished coup—but also shows how closely Nabokov read. He responds in his work not only to the fairy-tale Dane and the

---

24   Hanno Buddenbrooks's best friend is named Kai and disappears at the end in a snowstorm—like his prototype in Andersen's tale, who is whisked away by a sled. Arctic air from the realm of the Snow Queen also wafts on the Magic Mountain. See Maar, *Geister und Kunst*, passim.

25   Field noted that Nabokov's novel *King, Queen, Knave* took its title (if not its depiction of characters who are as two-dimensional as cards) from an Andersen fairy tale that was published in *Rul'*. (See Field, *Life and Art*, 114.)

26   *Pnin*, 89.

major author from Lübeck, but apparently even to the appropriation of the former by the latter. Literature can be a great ballroom resounding with echoes.

Or perhaps it's the Snow Queen's Crystal Chamber, which Lolita will visit too.[27] Nabokov explicitly called his novel a fairy tale. (It's no accident that it ends in "Elph's Stone" and begins in "Pixie," and no more an accident that Humbert gives his nymphet a deluxe volume of Andersen's *The Little Mermaid* for her thirteenth birthday.[28]) Andersen's most famous fairy tale not only made a profound impression on the young Thomas Mann.[29] Nabokov's work, too, is teeming with mermaids.[30] In *Lolita* he alludes to them only in passing, but that's just the beginning. His late novel *Ada* is a thinly veiled retelling of the sad fairy tale.

It's scarcely necessary to recite the story, which every child knows. The little mermaid rises to the surface of the sea on her fifteenth birthday and sees a ship with three masts on which there is music and song. Sailors are dancing on the deck. Through the cabin windows she glimpses the young prince with the black eyes whose birthday is being celebrated. When the ship sinks in a storm, she rescues the prince and falls in love with him. To attain the prince and an immortal soul, she visits the sea witch, exchanges her tail for human legs, and leaves the underwater kingdom. With every step she takes on her new legs she feels as if she were treading on sharp knives, but she can't complain, because the sea witch cut off her tongue in exchange for the legs. She lives mutely in the company of the prince, who is fond of her as a friend, but loves another woman, who he

---

27  See *Lolita*, 157. Humbert's trip to the North Pole, one of the least convincing passages in the novel (despite the Melville allusion), anticipates the motif. And as "The Frigid Queen," the Snow Queen ultimately makes a personal appearance. (Ibid., 166.) Alfred Appel provides a valuable overview of the fairy-tale motifs in Nabokov's works. In the foreword to his *Annotated Lolita*, he also cites Andersen's "The Shadow," to which *Lolita* and *Pale Fire* (with a protagonist named Shade) allude. (See *The Annotated Lolita*, 345–47 and lxi.) In "The Shadow" Andersen quotes Adelbert von Chamisso, then Mann quotes Andersen, and Nabokov quotes all three.

28  See *Lolita*, 174. For "Pixie" and "Elph's Stone," see *Selected Letters*, 413.

29  See Maar, *Geister und Kunst*, 85–93.

30  See Emily Collins, "Nabokov's *Lolita* and Andersen's *The Little Mermaid*," in *Nabokov Studies* 9 (2005), 77–100.

thinks saved him. The mermaid is barred from his bedroom. When the prince celebrates his wedding on a ship, the tale comes to a tragic finale. The little mermaid, who knows that she must die if the prince marries another, decides not to save herself and turn back into a mermaid by murdering the prince. She casts a final, passionate glance at the bridal pair after the wedding night and throws herself into the sea. Instead of dissolving into the foam, she rises to the daughters of the air, among whom she can obtain an immortal soul after hundreds of years through good deeds.[31]

How closely Nabokov cleaves to his model in *Ada* becomes apparent when the novel is superimposed over the Andersen tale. In *Ada*, too, the male object of desire appears in a sailor suit when Ada sees him for the first time.[32] Van and Ada are the lovers against whom the little mermaid Lucette has no chance. It is therefore fitting that Ada's sister is occasionally called a mermaid.[33] Like the little mermaid, Lucette is bitterly neglected; though everyone likes her, no one really takes her seriously. Her love for Prince Van is as ardent as it is hopeless. She remains the third wheel, suffers in silence like the mermaid, and shares with her a watery death.

The climax of *Ada* and of Nabokov's late work takes place on an ocean liner. Lucette has booked passage in order—at last, at last—to seduce Van, who cannot escape her on board. Her plan almost seems to be working, when his gaze falls upon the other woman: in a movie they are watching, Ada appears unexpectedly in a minor role. One look at Ada is enough to deter Van from the nocturnal rendezvous he and Lucette had arranged. Lucette, rejected and humiliated for the last time, throws herself over the railing into the black, tumultuous sea.[34] The messages she will

---

31 See http://hca.gilead.org.il/li_merma.html
32 See *Ada*, 149.
33 Ibid., 562 and passim.
34 Ibid., 474–95. The chapter is one of the most powerful in Nabokov's late work. There is also a dramatic love-triangle scene on a ship in *Pnin*. Here, too, the protagonist realizes that the love object will belong to another from now on, and falls into despair. Fortunately, Pnin doesn't throw himself overboard. But we understand why he doesn't find all that funny a certain newspaper cartoon with which his landlady, Joan Clements, tries to cheer him up. Perhaps it's better if he doesn't look too closely, for the erotic

convey to Ada as a daughter of the air constitute the most mysterious motif of the novel.[35]

The death of the little mermaid must have been intended as *Ada*'s climax from the beginning. Lucette's suicide on the ship lends a crucial balance to the whole novel, which would otherwise be nothing but a celebration of hedonism. The fairy-tale pattern is not imprinted merely on certain details, but rather on the entire plot. It is astounding that Nabokov simultaneously manages to keep one eye on the Lübeck cathedral.

Thomas Mann's great late work *Doctor Faustus* was met with much admiration in America. His protagonist, Adrian Leverkühn, the syphilitic composer who was intended to represent the demonic fate of the Germans (this allegorical structure alone could not but fill Nabokov with distaste)—this solitary, cold man who makes a pact with the devil and at the same time wears a crucifix—confesses in his madness to having been the little mermaid's lover. In his farewell speech to an uncomfortable audience, he even claims to have had a child with her. In actuality, outside of his delusion, Leverkühn had sexual contact with another woman, a Hungarian whore, whom he willingly allowed to infect him. She plays a role in his compositions as a ghostly cipher named Hetaera Esmeralda. Esmeralda and the mermaid are the only women with whom Leverkühn has sexual relations; they constitute the duality of the female Eros that Mann invokes in *Faustus*.[36]

Thus it is almost uncanny to stumble on the following passage in a letter in *Ada*: The sinful siblings Van and Ada write to Lucette after an erotic skirmish à *trois* that they're sorry to have "inveigled our Esmeralda and mermaid in a naughty prank." Esmeralda and mermaid—the coupling comes directly from Thomas Mann.[37] As if to make the genealogy official,

---

motif would surely pain him: a cat and a shipwrecked mariner on a desert island see a mermaid—the cat imagines her in its thought bubble as all fish; the mariner desires her as all woman. (See *Pnin*, 47–61.)

35  The "mermaid's message" plays a decisive role when the love between Van and Ada enters a new phase. This message is clearly from Lucette, who wants to spare Ada her own fate. (See *Ada*, 562, and Boyd, *Nabokov's Pale Fire*, 285, n10.)

36  Mann, *Doctor Faustus*, 246, 524.

37  *Ada*, 421.

Nabokov permits himself one of those name jokes that often made Edmund Wilson sigh. He puns on Helen Lowe-Porter—Mann's translator, who transported *Doktor Faustus* into English. The translator of an author named "Eelmann" belongs to a firm "of Packers & Porters," Ada says mockingly, and then she bemoans the fact that poor Lucette has to study this Eelmann and the "three terrible Toms" in her literature course. In a note Nabokov himself breaks down the allusion.[38] It almost seems as if he cannot bridle his resentment, as if it were holding the reins. And that raises the question of whether this resentment was based solely on aesthetic disapproval; if not, what else could be feeding it?

This question might be related to another: Why, of all possible brides, does Mann give his composer the chaste mermaid? The novel itself does not reveal much in this regard—Leverkühn had always been fond of this fairy tale, we learn, and his stabbing headaches remind him of the "pains like slashing knives" that Andersen's mermaid was forced to suffer.[39] But Leverkühn's creator had better reasons for choosing this character. He knew a few things about the fairy-tale Dane.

Mermaids prior to Andersen have in common that they're cold and soulless. They catch a human man to be their husband in order to gain an immortal soul. Andersen's undine also wants an immortal soul, but the actual reason for her ascent into the human world is her silent love for the prince. In this fairy tale, Andersen was writing in code about his passion for Edvard Collin, the true love of his life. Like the fairy-tale prince, Collin tolerated the presence of the unusual old maid as a good friend in his house, but reserved his bedroom for real women. *The Little Mermaid* was written when Collin got married. Andersen fled from the wedding and wrote his most famous tale.

It was a long time before readers realized that he had woven into his story a little scene in which the kernel of truth was concealed. The prince

---

38   "O'Neill, Thomas Mann and his translator tangle in this paragraph," explains Nabokov's anagrammatic sister Vivian Darkbloom in the "Notes to Ada." (See Ibid., 403, 602.)

39   Mann, *Doctor Faustus*, 246.

has a page's dress made for the mermaid so she can accompany him on horseback. She could have ridden sidesaddle and in a dress, if need be, but it was precisely for the sake of this ambivalence that Andersen conceived the scene. The mermaid is an androgynous male who loves another man and wants to be close to him, even if it brings him nothing but torments. He cannot speak of these torments, for the witch has cut off his tongue. When the prince asks her about herself, the mermaid can only make eyes at him, "but she could not speak."[40] In the volume of Andersen's fairy tales preserved in the Thomas Mann Archives in Zurich, there is a little red cross right at this point in the text, after "but she could not speak," marking the middle of the page. The fellow sufferer knew of what the maiden could not speak. [41]

And Nabokov knew it too. Andersen's secret was revealed in 1901 in a journal that broke the public silence regarding the phenomenon of male homosexual love: the *Yearbook for Sexual Intermediates* published by Magnus Hirschfeld. The long article "H. C. Andersen: Proof of his Homosexuality" gathered all the evidence of Andersen's double life. His fiction testified clearly enough to his erotic inclinations. "A pair of brown eyes" always had to circumvent the fact that they did not belong to a "her," but rather to a "him." Even his adulation of the Swedish Nightingale was just one of his typical protective maneuvers in the face of a suspicious public. The article even cited a Danish writer arrested for sex crimes who provided unmentionable details about his relationship with Andersen. The author of the article found additional reason to believe that Andersen hadn't abstained from acting out on his sexual proclivities in light of statements made by still-living homosexuals.[42]

Presumably, Nabokov knew the *Yearbook* well, as someone very close to him had been published in it. In 1903 an essay titled "Homosexuality in

---

40  See http://hca.gilead.org.il/li_merma.html
41  See Maar, *Geister und Kunst*, 94–103. As a curiosity, it may be noted that a quite peculiar motif of *The Magic Mountain*, an alphabet consisting of twenty-five instead of twenty-six letters, also surfaces in Nabokov's work—in *Bend Sinister*, in which the missing letter is identified. It is *I*, the self.
42  See *Jahrbuch für sexuelle Zwischenstufen* III (1901), 92–98.

the Russian Penal Code" had appeared. The author was a professor of criminal law at the Imperial Law School in St. Petersburg: Vladimir Nabokoff.[43]

---

43 See *Jahrbuch für sexuelle Zwischenstufen* IV (1903), 1159–71. Books by "German sexologists" are also mentioned in *Ada* (131).

# 3

# SODOM

*I felt the heat of her limbs through her rough tomboy clothes*
*(Lolita)*

The night before the most traumatic event of his life, Nabokov had as usual chatted a bit with his father before bed. The conversation turned to the "strange, abnormal inclinations" of Vladimir's younger brother, Sergei. Sighing, they'd discussed the incomprehensibility of the case.[1]

It takes exactly five pages for the subject to turn up in his work. In Nabokov's debut novel, *Mary*, a male couple appears in the second chapter, two ballet dancers who giggle like little girls, powder their noses, knock on the door with a "velvety-soft and feminine" tap, and pout like women. The others notice their "odd affected manner," but "in all honesty no one could blame this harmless couple for being as happy as a pair of ringdoves."[2]

No one? Some quiet doubts may arise when one surveys Nabokov's oeuvre. The ballet dancers in *Mary* lead a parade of homosexuals that proceeds all the way to *Ada*. It would be an exaggeration to say that the author's sympathies lie with them. If Nabokov took action against unwelcome critics in the manner of Heine against Platen and called his influential enemy Georgy Adamovich—who, according to Nabokov, had only two passions in life, Russian poetry and French sailors—"Uranski"

---

1   See Boyd, *The Russian Years,* 192.
2   See *Mary,* 5, 37, 63, 64.     .

or "Sodomovich," that's all well and good, or not so well and good.[3] But how he treats male homosexual love in his fiction almost shows symptoms of compulsion.

To give just a few examples, since the complete list would be too tedious: In an early draft of *The Defense*, his third novel, Nabokov planned for the protagonist, Luzhin, to see a black beard on his wife. The final version was shorn of the homosexual motif.[4] The narrator of his next novel, *The Eye*, is suspected of being a "sexual lefty."[5] In *Glory* the Cambridge tutor Moon is a homosexual; the protagonist, Martin, is put off by his pawing hands.[6] The executioner Pierre in *Invitation to a Beheading* is the type of homosexual who boasts of his conquests of women. The repugnant writer in the story "Spring in Fialta," a man who is always ready with a "poisonous pun," is "eclectic"—that is, bisexual.[7] In *Laughter in the Dark* the villain feigns disgust for the tender sex so as to throw dust into his rival's eyes.[8] In *Bend Sinister* the dictator Paduk,

---

3   The influential poet and critic Georgy Adamovich had long reviewed Sirin/ Nabokov's poems harshly. Nabokov's revenge was cunning: he published poems under the pseudonym Vasily Shishkov, and Adamovich sang their praises—a new poet had been born. In the story "Vasily Shishkov," published shortly thereafter, Nabokov revealed the pseudonym and held Adamovich up to ridicule. The denigrating name-calling shows a Nabokov with less command of himself. *Uranism* was a contemporary term for homosexuality. (See Field, *Life and Art*, 132–35; also Lev Grossman, "The Gay Nabokov," Salon.com, May 17, 2000.)

4   See Field, *Life and Art*, 132.

5   *The Eye*, 84. Nabokov's most Dostoyevskian novel is the first that plays with the unreliable narrator. A man survives an attempted suicide, dissociates from his earlier self, and observes as a neutral eye how this earlier self is judged by others. The narrative trick is that even though we suspect the identity of the narrator with the chameleon-like "he," our suspicions are not unambiguously confirmed until the end.

6   *Glory*, 97.

7   *Stories*, 420, 425.

8   The cuckold falls for the false confession and remarks politely: "In a shopkeeper, it would repel me, but in a painter, it's quite different—quite likeable, in fact, and romantic—romance coming from Rome." (See *Laughter in the Dark*, 166.) *Laughter in the Dark* summarizes its plot in the first paragraph, and the somewhat false fairy-tale tone already shows that it's not the best Nabokov who begins here: "Once upon a time there lived in Berlin, Germany, a man called Albinus. He was rich, respectable, happy; one day he abandoned his wife for the sake of a youthful mistress; he loved; was not loved; and his life ended in disaster." Betrayed by Margot, the evil girl with whom he's

known as the Toad, is a stutterer and a homosexual in disguise. Into the forties, there's something obsessive about the association of homosexuality with the malevolent in Nabokov's work.

Hermann, the megalomaniac in *Despair*, is the most malevolent of them all. Without himself being entirely aware of it, he is sexually attracted to his murder victim, Felix, whom he at one point calls his brother. During their first encounter, Felix pockets Hermann's ominous silver pencil—the same one that Hans Castorp borrows from Hippe, his schoolmate and the object of his erotic desire, in *The Magic Mountain*. Before Hermann shares a hotel room with Felix, lies with him almost under the same blanket and dreams of "telltale stains of a slimy nature," he tells us that his fancy runs riot, "and that rather disgustingly." It's scarcely necessary for Nabokov to have his narrator write stories "in the Oscar Wilde style" or to have him mention the sodomistic resonances of his own tale in order to play on the ambiguity of the sentence with which Hermann prepares to commit murder: "In the cold wood there stood in front of me a naked man. Incredibly fast ... I undressed."[9] That the amoral

---

fallen in love, Albinus loses his eyesight in an accident and must listen helplessly in the darkness, in which inexplicable things happen. Margot's lover is secretly living with them, and the defenseless Albinus is mocked and tormented by him until help arrives from outside—help, however, that hastens his end. When he attempts to take revenge, Albinus is shot by Margot—the mythical serpent who, like Keats's Lamia, vanishes afterward into thin air. With the love-triangle story Nabokov again, as so often, casts a sidelong glance at Proust. Its structure resembles the tale of Swann with Odette and Charlus. Like Swann, only mistakenly, Albert believes himself to be safe with the harmless homosexual friend Rex pretends to be. The name Albert is itself indebted to Proust, whose Albertine will reenact Swann's tale of woe with Marcel. Nabokov augments Swann's jealous agonies through the theme of blindness. He also appropriates other little motifs from Proust's *In Search of Lost Time,* like that of peeking through one's fingers, from the scene of the grandmother's death. Out of the housemaid Françoise he makes a German Frieda. For the prominent role of Proust in Nabokov, see 109, n. 30.

9   See *Despair*, 66, 14, 97, 85, 108, 159, 168–69. With this bizarre beast of a book, "a rhinoceros in a world of humming birds," as he himself called it, Nabokov brilliantly continues his series of unreliable narrators. (See *Selected Letters*, 17.) For one thing, the megalomaniacal criminal Hermann has a strained relationship with truth. On top of that, he is unpardonably naïve. From the little incongruities, the contradictions, and the muttered asides, the reader must deduce all that escapes Hermann or is deliberately withheld from him. Like Albinus in *Laughter in the Dark*, he doesn't suspect that his wife

artist is mirrored in a homosexual brother-figure also anticipates Humbert's relation to Quilty.

In "Solus Rex," a chapter from an unfinished novel written in 1939, "ultra-urningism," as it's called there, moves from the shadowy corners to center stage.[10] This tale contains the least-veiled homosexual scene in Nabokov's work (in early publications it was replaced by an ellipsis). Prince Adulf, the promiscuous heir to the throne, masturbates the acrobat Guldving. Witness to this scene is the naïve protagonist K, who is shocked and nauseated. The lewd prince, notorious for his seduction of young-sters, tries to draw K into his circle.[11] Let us note in passing that it is a relative, the son of K's uncle, who is inclined toward these sexual abuses.

And let us also note in passing that Prince Adulf doesn't just happen to have that name. In 1939 no character in a novel just happens to be called Adulf. A conspicuously Germanic air wafts in the Nordic and extremely unappealing world of "Solus Rex," no less than in the still more horrible world of the 1945 novel *Bend Sinister.*[12] Even the external plot of "Solus Rex" seems to have been inspired by a German court scandal, the famous Eulenburg Affair.[13] The novel into which "Solus Rex" later evolved,

---

is shamelessly betraying him. He takes notice only of details at the periphery of his field of vision, but does not recognize their significance—that his wife's missing lipstick is found in her cousin's shirtpocket; that she quite naturally uses his hairbrush; or that the same cousin, when she undresses on the beach, flees with the explanation that he's going to search for edible toadstools. Nothing about all this strikes Hermann as odd. He thinks only of himself and his immortal artwork—in a novel in which he deals in an artfully hallucinatory fashion with themes from Nabokov's life, as if he himself and not his rival had eaten those toadstools. One of those themes is the homosexuality of which he himself is not quite aware.

10   See *Stories*, 541.

11   Ibid., 536. See also *Selected Letters*, 481–82.

12   The language spoken in "Solus Rex" is a sort of Scandinavian Old German, the king's wife is called *husmuder*, and oak wardrobes adorn the castle chamber. In *Bend Sinister* an "early luncheon" is called *frishtik* and a failure *schlapp*, an officer commands "*Heraus, Mensch, marsch*," and the brand of pencils is Eberhard Faber. (See *Bend Sinister*, 220, 199, 125, 148.)

13   "Solus Rex" revolves around a court scandal that distinctly recalls a 1908 trial that shook the German Empire. Nabokov père, the expert on homosexuality in criminal law, was undoubtedly familiar with the scandal. The journalist Maximilian Harden had accused Prince von Eulenburg, adviser to the Kaiser, of violating Paragraph 175, which

published in 1962, also has a Germanic subtext: the labyrinthine *Pale Fire*, which many consider Nabokov's masterpiece, shows even more clearly than the 1939 fragment how intimately Nabokov knew that which repelled him. His richly interspersed allusions to German Romanticism combine into a nexus of ideas that is not so different from the German cultural complex of the despised *Faustus* author.[14] Only the angle of illumination was different—what the one loved into his old age provoked nothing but cold contempt in the other.

This contempt also figures in the portrayal of Kinbote in *Pale Fire*. Charles Kinbote, who loves German Romanticism, is the antithesis of the aging professor and poet John Shade, whose dignified, beautiful poem *Pale Fire*, written in heroic couplets in the manner of Pope, forms the core of the novel. Kinbote, Shade's neighbor and university colleague, adds the flesh, the voluminous and insane commentary. Insane because Kinbote lives under the delusion of being the exiled and hunted king of a Nordic kingdom called Zembla—a delusion that he projects onto John Shade's poem, which is devoted to entirely different themes: God and the world, his daughter's suicide and his ensuing grief (the most moving passage in Nabokov's work). Shade's poem is left unfinished when he falls victim to a misdirected assassination: an escaped convict shoots him, believing him to be the judge who had sentenced him. (In Kinbote's fantasy the killer is the Zemblan assassin Gradus and the bullet was actually meant for him, the exiled king.) Shade's widow turns over the manuscript of *Pale Fire* to her strange neighbor in a moment of gratitude. Kinbote will annotate it with his paranoid notes until his suicide, which lies beyond the novel but

---

prohibited homosexuality. In "Solus Rex" Prince Adulf is undergoing a similar trial. Nabokov might also have heard the rumors that the Kaiser himself belonged to the circle around Eulenburg. They were no less widespread than the later speculations about the secret predilections of the German Adulf. One can find all these motifs, with slight distortions, in the story that ultimately never grew into a novel.

14  Nabokov alludes to Richard Wagner, Ludwig II, and even the mythologist Johann Jakob Bachofen, whose work on mother-right was a key text for Thomas Mann, an influence that is evident in the Joseph novel. The three cruel Bachofen sisters who appear in *Bend Sinister* and who follow Linda Bachofen in "Solus Rex" point to Nabokov's acquaintance with this Romantic–Germanic complex.

is clearly foreshadowed in it. In actuality, as one can infer from certain slips in his commentary and index, Kinbote seems to be a Russian named Botkin who is shunned at the university. But in Botkin/Kinbote's confused mind, this truth only rarely rises to the surface.

Of course—as one is almost obliged to say after the above enumeration—of course Charles Kinbote is a homosexual too.[15] And of course he therefore cannot be an appealing character. He is a pushy neighbor who sorely tests the Shades' patience. He spies on the couple; he is jealous, annoying, and meddlesome; he lies.

On the other hand—and it's the first time there is an "on the other hand"—Kinbote is subtly linked to Shade's brooding, homely, and tragically departed daughter, to whom her father devotes all his love. Not much but a little of this warmth is also shed on the lonely, anxious, and religious Romantic who is perhaps inspired by the dead daughter and shares an end with her. Something has shifted since the early novels in which the "uranists" were merely disgusting or evil, or both. The emotional mix has become more complex. Kinbote is not nice, but he's a poor dog, and a few sparks of pity glimmer for him.

In the series that began with the effeminate ballet dancers, Kinbote is the last and most prominent representative. It is all the more revealing that a decisive nuance is missing when one labels him a homosexual. In a very subtle fashion, Kinbote's predilection is still more narrowly defined. He doesn't love men, but boys.[16] Therein lies his chief sin, in his own view. A hidden theme of the novel is pedophilia. In other words: even the flames of *Pale Fire* are still licking at the theme of *Lolita*.[17]

---

15    In this, Kinbote takes after his father, who was responsible for dubbing the capital of Zembla "Uranograd." (See *Pale Fire*, 102.)

16    See Boyd, *Nabokov's Pale Fire*, 96. Boyd deciphers a sensual, suicidal statement by Kinbote as referring to "a boy's tight little scrotum," which Nabokov confirms in a letter to his French translator, not without adding, "Dr. Kinbote is not a nice man." (Ibid., 271.)

17    There are considerable similarities between *Lolita* and *Pale Fire* in terms of narrative tone. Above all, there is a resemblance in the ecstasies and breakdowns at the end of a passage, when Humbert and Kinbote, who share a forbidden desire, are exhausted, dead-tired of the cesspool of sin, and can no longer go on. And both fall repeatedly out of the fiction. "Well, folks, I guess many in this fine hall are as hungry and thirsty as me,

## Lolita in Tomboy Clothes

But isn't *Lolita* about a man who loves a young girl? That's one story, but the novel apparently wants to tell several simultaneously—hence its extraordinary prismatic quality. Humbert Humbert yearns for young girls, not boys—but if that sentence were entirely accurate, certain thematic strands should not be in the book; nor should they be so meticulously interwoven.

The parade did not circumvent Nabokov's magnum opus. According to old habit, it is flanked by a few minor characters. As a masculine woman in "Solus Rex" drives a motorcycle with her husband in a sidecar, in Humbert's neighborhood lives the female couple *Les*ter and Fa*bian*.[18] A more important and quite vivid minor character is Humbert's chess partner Gaston, a French professor who decorates his room with photographs of Gide, Proust, Tchaikovsky, and Nijinsky and absentmindedly asks Humbert about the well-being of his little girls: *"Et toutes vos fillettes, elles vont bien?"* In his eyes Lolita, to whom he never pays attention and who's always dressed differently, has fanned out into multiple girls. Gaston, in Humbert's unkind words a "glum repulsive fat old invert," vanishes from the novel after a *sale histoire* in Naples.[19] His theme, however, lies at its heart.

Humbert loves nymphets, certain girls between the ages of nine and fourteen who seem to him to constitute their own gender—similar to the "third sex" that Hirschfeld considered his uranists to be. He pokes fun at the psychiatrists on whose file cards he is described as potentially homosexual.[20] But that doesn't prevent him from praising Lolita's boyish hips and her "beautiful boy-knees" or tenderly calling her *mon petit*.[21] His little

---

and I'd better stop, folks, right here. Yes, better stop. My notes and self are petering out. Gentlemen, I have suffered very much, and more than any of you can imagine." Humbert could just as well have spoken this last sentence to his jurors. (See *Pale Fire*, 300.)

18   See *Lolita*, 179. Humbert is to blame for the name joke, but Nabokov is coresponsible for the cliché of Lester's short hair.

19   Ibid., 181–83.

20   Ibid., 34.

21   Ibid., 22, 120, 243.

boy sometimes slips into the wrong clothing—another classic camouflage signal. Like the little mermaid, who unfortunately can go riding only in a page's dress, the girl who receives the Andersen book as a gift likes to wear a boy's shirt.[22]

Does Nabokov give his heroine, by way of these scattered but systematic hints, a double life as a boy? In his last, unfinished novel, *The Original of Laura*, he will bring the motif much more drastically into focus. Here Lolita's descendant, named Aurora Lee, appears to the protagonist in a wet dream. He strokes and fondles her, reaches between her thighs from behind, and feels there the "sweat-stuck folds of a long scrotum and then, further in front, the droop of a short member."[23]—Oops. The secret that in *Lolita* is still artfully sidestepped has been revealed.

To this art belongs Nabokov's strategy of making Humbert's proclivity ambiguous—for can the lover of a girl in which a boy might be hiding be particularly straight? Nabokov achieves this ambiguity with a little trick: the merging of one character into another. Humbert is not alone; he has a doppelgänger or a split identity. From the opening pages on, it is made almost too plain that there is no clear-cut separation between the characters of Humbert and the demonic Clare Quilty. This is already revealed in the foreword by the fictitious Dr. John Ray Jr. Just as Vladimir Nabokov writes a sort of biography of Humbert Humbert, so too does his anagrammatic doppelgänger, Vivian Darkbloom, write a biography of Clare Quilty—in the view of critics who have perused the manuscript, her best book.[24] Lolita's two corrupters not only outwardly resemble each other, but also share similar tastes, down to their purple

---

22  Ibid., 46, 255.

23  *The Original of Laura*, [101], [102], [103] (indicates index card number). Dr. Wild, "an authority on dreams," hastens to add that "this was no homosexual manifestation but a splendid example of terminal gynandrism." (Ibid., [103].)

24  *Lolita*, 4. The other function of this passage was to smuggle in the author's own name in case of anonymous publication, as was initially planned. But the name didn't necessarily have to be linked to Quilty. Appel speaks of Clare Quilty as Humbert's "grotesque alter ego and parodic double." (*The Annotated Lolita*, 321.) In light of the various little chronological inconsistencies and Quilty's seeming predictions of future events, Boyd wonders whether he might not even be Humbert's secret stage director. (See *American Years*, 246–49.)

dressing gowns, and are sinful brothers in spirit.[25] Quilty is not only Humbert's rival and mortal enemy, but also his grotesque shadow. Ultimately, Humbert perceives himself and his alter ego as two Humberts.[26] The other Humbert parodies and casts into relief what Humbert veils with rhetoric and wit. But what is striking about the monstrous Quilty, aside from the fact that he likes to seduce young girls? His first name, Clare, appears ambiguous in itself. Since it can pass as female, Lolita shrewdly employs it as a diversion: she lulls Humbert into the belief that the author of the play in which she has a part is an old woman.

And in a way he is. In the grand finale Nabokov doesn't hold back in his portrayal of Quilty as what Proust would call a *tante*. If the word did not exist, one would have to invent it for this scene: in the face of death, Quilty turns into a queen. Threatened by Humbert, he complains in his "strange feminine manner" and tempts him with photographs of more than eight hundred male organs. On the run, he scurries and makes "a feminine 'ah!'" when hit by a bullet from the pistol, which aches to be discharged and is described clearly enough as phallic.[27] And so the two wrestle: "I rolled over him. We rolled over me. They rolled over him. We rolled over us."[28] This thinly veiled homosexual act is foreshadowed by Quilty's pseudonyms in the hotel guestbooks that "ejaculate" their meaning in Humbert's face.[29] Dying, Quilty rises like the mad Nijinsky, who had already adorned Gaston's bachelor pad.[30] When he finally collapses—to the delight of the flesh flies, which can't believe their luck—Humbert's hour has also struck. A few weeks later he is a dead man.

---

25   *Lolita*, 57, 246, 295.

26   See ibid., 217. Humbert also occasionally refers to Quilty as a brother whom he wants to destroy. (Ibid., 247.)

27   Ibid., 296, 302, 303, 292. Nabokov wrote about the "phallic implications" of a pistol in relation to Charlie Chaplin, who was threatened with such a weapon by his lover Joan Barry. (See *Dear Bunny, Dear Volodya*, 142.)

28   *Lolita*, 299.

29   Ibid., 250.

30   Ibid., 302, 181.

## Trapp, trapp, trapp

But what's all this about? Lolita may not be unambiguously female, Humbert's doppelgänger is a woman in a satyr's body—why this rumbling below the surface of the novel? We cannot come up with a satisfactory explanation if we don't take into account another story that *Lolita* may want to tell us. It, too, is about pedophilia, but of the homosexual variety. The child that fell victim to it was not named Dolores, but Vladimir.

As we learn from *Speak, Memory*, the author had a homosexual uncle, Ruka, who often took the nine-year-old Nabokov on his knee after lunch. This uncle, who later left Nabokov his estate, would fondle him "with crooning sounds and fancy endearments" until his father called from the veranda, *"Basile, on vous attend"*—obviously to defuse the uncomfortable situation. It's hard not to think of the scene in which Humbert takes Lolita on his lap and attains his first forbidden pleasure. In *Ada*, too, there are echoes of the autobiographical episode: the nine-year-old heroine is always being indecently groped by the family's painter friend; the palpable general sense of relief when the pawing comes to an end seems to recall the moment in *Speak, Memory*.[31]

Humbert, too, repeatedly mentions an ominous uncle—one wonders why, since this fellow contributes nothing to the plot. He is a "rather repulsive" Swiss wine dealer named Gustave Trapp, whose chief function seems to be to remind Humbert of other men.[32] The thematic chain is quite strange, as cryptic as it is elaborate. Humbert's doppelgänger has an uncle too, the dentist Ivor Quilty, whom the murderous Humbert tracks down in Ramsdale in order to find out where the nephew lives. This uncle, an avowed nude bather, reminds Humbert fleetingly of his own. But Quilty, too, reminds him of Gustave, as he remarks with a "come to think of it" when he first encounters his adversary, still a stranger to him, leering at Lolita in the hotel. His train of thought has an obscene undercurrent; it is the lecherous gaze of the stranger that brings to mind his uncle, who was also a great admirer of *le découvert*. Quilty will sign one of

31  See *Speak, Memory*, 68, and *Ada*, 111–12.
32  *Lolita*, 290, 218, 139.

his guestbook entries as "G. Trapp."[33] And there is someone else who reminds Humbert of his uncle: Gaston, who ends up in depravity in Naples, whose name he mixes up with Gustave's.[34] Both men share the epithet "repulsive."

All this points in one direction. The uncle's name itself is not without undertones. It not only suggests a snare, *la trappe*, but also echoes lines from Gottfried August Bürger's ballad "Lenore"—*"Und außen, horch! ging's trapp, trapp, trapp"* ("And outside, hark! It went trapp, trapp, trapp")—which Nabokov often quoted and was just as fond as Humbert of relating to riding in the figurative sense.[35] And so we come back to riding on the lap—this time, however, an uncle's lap.

Lolita is eating an apple when she triggers Humbert's orgasm. We need not see in this the biblical fall, which expels the child from the paradise of innocence, the primal scene that Nabokov recreated in his writing throughout his life. Yet one cannot help noticing the thematic relations that radiate from this scene.[36]

---

33  Ibid., 138–39, 251. The guestbook signature is one of the novel's many little fictional breaches, for Quilty cannot know the name.

34  See ibid., 202.

35  "Now hop-hop-hop, Lenore," Humbert quotes from Bürger's ballad, which is indeed ambiguous: "His sweetheart tucked in her skirt, jumped and vaulted up nimbly on to the horse; she twined her lily-white hands round the dear horseman; and hey, hey, hop, hop, hop away they went at a rousing gallop ..." (*The Penguin Book of German Verse*, 185.) In a letter to Alfred Appel dated April 2, 1967, Nabokov refers specifically to the "irresistible line": *Und außen, horch! ging's trapp, trapp, trapp.* (See *Lolita*, 207, and *Selected Letters*, 409.) The subtext of German Classicism in *Lolita*, which is often overlooked, is astonishingly wide-ranging: with Fräulein von Kulp (read: Kalb) and Charlotte, with Schiller, Werther, Erlkönig, and Bürger, about whom Nabokov knew as much as he did about Kotzebue or Fouqué.

36  In *Solving Nabokov's Lolita Riddle* Joanne Morgan attempts to demonstrate numerical—not to say numerological—codes that Nabokov smuggled into his works. In *Lolita* the numbers 342 (read: "three for two") and their mirror image, 243, play a prominent role. This is not only the house number of Lolita's Ramsdale address, but also the room number in the Enchanted Hunters. Humbert registers at 342 hotels in search of the escaped Lolita. Now for the climax: Nabokov writes in the first edition of *Speak, Memory: A Memoir* (1951) of a valuable cane that he inherited from a great-uncle. This detail is on page 178. In the expanded version of 1966–67 he specifies that it was Uncle Ruka who bequeathed him the cane when he was a child. This addition is—in accordance with the author's instructions, claims Morgan—on page 243. Unfortunately,

We recall the references in "Solus Rex" to impermissible abuses in the family. In debates about *Pale Fire*, speculations circulate that Shade was sexually abused by his aunt and that the secret theme of the novel is incest.[37] The incest motif already turns up as a hidden element in "The Potato Elf," and it meanders inconspicuously through Nabokov's whole oeuvre. To give an example: the teenage lover of the protagonist, Albinus, in *Laughter in the Dark* is mistaken for his daughter one time too many. That is another way in which she is a precursor to Lolita, whose corrupter has, in lieu of a family life, only the "parody of incest" to offer her.[38]

The force with which the theme breaks through to the surface in the author's old age is as astonishing as it is mysterious. Like Thomas Mann, who in his late novel *The Holy Sinner* has brother sleep with sister and mother with son, Nabokov devotes the magnum opus of his later years wholly to incest. Van and Ada are siblings, which doesn't diminish their passion for each other. On the contrary, in the depiction of this passion

---

Morgan loses credibility when she deciphers the name Adam Krug as an anagram of "mad Ruka," which, even leaving aside other reasons, cannot be correct because the *g* is missing, and anagrams, like pregnancies, exist either completely or not at all.

37    The crucial debates take place on the Internet Listserv NABOKV-L [*sic*]. For how Pynchon readers contributed to a rereading of *Pale Fire* in terms of incest, see the NABOKV-L archive.

38    *Lolita*, 287. In another, more subtle way, *Laughter in the Dark* draws attention to the underlying web of forbidden pleasure and guilt. It is a tiny detail that does not appear in *Camera Obscura*, the earlier version of the novel. Not only does Albinus's wife leave him, but his child dies of pneumonia. Not that he could have done anything about it—thematically, however, he is linked almost imperceptibly to her death. Nabokov needs only one sentence to accomplish this: after his daughter dies, Albinus leaves the house. At the front door below he meets a snow-covered man, who is let in by a woman. This fellow is the woman's lover. He whistles four notes from *Siegfried* on the street to signal to the woman to come down; it is the same whistle that Albinus's daughter knows from her father and that impelled her to open the window and expose herself to the deadly night air. The messenger or bringer of death makes his farewell rounds after his work has been accomplished, and Nabokov once again interweaves the motifs of secret love and paternal guilt with the faint hint of incest. (Interestingly, the *Siegfried* motif appears only in the later version.) And that's what makes things thorny: Albinus symbolically exchanges one daughter for the other; he sacrifices the true daughter for the false one. (*Laughter in the Dark*, 175–76, 158–59.)

Nabokov gives rein to an opulence that surpasses even that of *Lolita*. Do certain inhibitions fall away in the face of approaching death? Is something exposed that was previously camouflaged, or does incest camouflage something else altogether? At French railroad crossings a sign often warns, "*Un train peut en cacher un autre.*" Unfortunately, there are no such signs in literature. The question of which train is hiding which is already tricky enough in *The Holy Sinner*. With late Nabokov one must surrender in the face of it. There is one figure, in any case, who is not missing from the Satanic Eden in which brother and sister live out their earthly delights: the pederastic uncle.[39]

His *trapp, trapp, trapp* is still ringing in our ears from *Lolita*, where it pointed to a subterranean story in the novel—a story more concealed than revealed, which doesn't mean that the story on the surface might not ultimately be the deepest.

But before we come back to it, we turn once again to Nabokov's brother, who was not so much a thorn in his side as a small, festering wound, which he dabbed again and again with the iodine of art.

## Sergei, No. 28631

Sergei Nabokov's life was ill-starred. His older brother, the firstborn, was their mother's favorite. The second son already had it hard as an embryo. During the pregnancy Elena Nabokov was under great strain and distress; her parents were ill and died a year after Sergei's birth. The child developed quite differently than her preferred son. Sergei was shy and awkward, had a terrible stutter, and lacked the charisma that Vladimir already exuded at an early age. The brothers' relationship was difficult from the start. Even as children "there was always a sort of aversion" between them, their sister recalled.[40] The uneasiness can also be sensed in Nabokov's autobiography. For various reasons, he confesses in a very

---

39  See *Ada*, 233. For the symbolism of incest in *Ada*, see also Michael Wood, who perceives in it "an extreme figure for a lurking taboo on outright sexual joy." ("Nabokov's Late Fiction" in *The Cambridge Companion to Nabokov*, 209.)
40  Grossman, "The Gay Nabokov."

despondent passage, he found it "inordinately hard" to speak about his brother. He hints at one of these reasons when he ruefully recalls committing a serious indiscretion as a youth: he found a page from Sergei's diary and showed it to his tutor, who showed it to his father. This diary page "provided a retroactive clarification of certain oddities of behavior on his part."[41]

Sergei had to withdraw from the famous Tenishev School. His diary had revealed that he was unhappily in love with boys. Though his father as a jurist had opposed the criminalization of homosexuality, he wasn't pleased when the problem began to manifest itself in his own house.[42] The subject was passed over in silence, but the father inwardly distanced himself from Sergei. His favorite son, who had snitched on his brother, did the same. Though Vladimir studied with Sergei in Cambridge, he didn't have much to do with him off the tennis court. "No two brothers could have been less alike," was the view of contemporary witnesses.[43] Sergei loved music, particularly that of Richard Wagner, and joined the Catholic Church—both were alien to the older brother, who was unmusical and averse to all churches. After Cambridge they parted ways. Not until the late thirties did they meet occasionally in Paris, where Sergei had moved after a brief stay in. Berlin and where he was connected to Diaghilev, Cocteau, and Gertrude Stein. According to one woman's impression from those years, he was the nicest and funniest of all the Nabokovs.[44] Vladimir tried after a fashion to come to terms with the fact

---

41   *Speak, Memory*, 257–58.
42   There were several homosexual relatives in the family, not only Ruka, who himself had a stutter (as if to confirm theories of a genetic leap from the uncle).
43   "Vladimir was the young *homme du monde*—handsome, romantic in looks, something of a snob and a gay charmer—Serge was the dandy, an aesthete and balletomane … [He] was tall and very thin. He was very blond and his tow-colored hair usually fell in a lock over his left eye. He suffered from a serious speech impediment, a terrible stutter. Help would only confuse him, so one had to wait until he could say what was on his mind, and it was usually worth hearing … He attended all the Diaghilev premieres wearing a flowing black theater cape and carrying a pommeled cane." (Lucie Léon Noël in Grossman, "The Gay Nabokov.")
44   "Nicolas' son Ivan is now in his 60s, too young to really remember Sergei, but he remembers his mother's account of him. According to her, Sergei was 'the nicest of all

that his brother had lived with a man since the end of the twenties—and what's more, a German-speaking man, the rich Austrian aristocrat Hermann Thieme (a first name that we recognize from the novel *Despair*).[45] When Vladimir fled from the German invasion of Paris in 1940, he was unable to say good-bye to Sergei, who, when he found his brother gone, "had to stutter his astonishment to an indifferent concierge," as Nabokov puts it in *Speak, Memory*.[46]

The following year, after moving back to Berlin, Sergei was arrested by the Gestapo on charges of homosexuality. After four months, he managed to be released, but remained under surveillance. Ironically, speaking out vehemently was ultimately the stutterer's undoing. Among friends and colleagues he sharply criticized Hitler, was denounced, arrested, and sent to the Neuengamme concentration camp. Of the hundred thousand prisoners there—who were, among other things, subjected to medical experiments—less than half survived. Homosexuals were singled out for particularly cruel treatment. Sergei Nabokov, prisoner no. 28631, demonstrated heroic altruism. In 1945, three months before the liberation of the camp, he died a miserable death.[47]

One can imagine the mix of emotions with which Nabokov confronted the fact that this strange other self, who had always stood in his

---

the Nabokovs ... a sweet, funny man ... much nicer, much more dependable and much funnier than all the rest of them.'" (Ibid.) Incidentally, Sergei provides a footnote to the never-ending Heine–Platen polemic: he complained that Vladimir and Véra's son was not only spoiled, but also frightfully Jewish-looking. (See Schiff, *Véra*, 99.)

45   Nabokov's letter to Véra after his first encounter with Hermann shows much goodwill, followed by the unavoidable "All the same": "The husband, I must admit, is very pleasant, quiet, not at all the pederast type, attractive face and manner. All the same I felt rather uncomfortable, especially when one of their friends came up, red-lipped and curly." (See Grossman, "The Gay Nabokov.")

46   *Speak, Memory*, 258.

47   See Boyd, *The American Years*, 88–89, and Grossman, "The Gay Nabokov." The latter also mentions Sergei's possible involvement in a plot to hide a British pilot. "Sergei's conduct in the camp was nothing less than heroic. Nicolas Nabokov's son Ivan says that after the war, survivors from Neuengamme would telephone his family out of the blue—they were the only Nabokovs in the book—just to talk about Sergei. 'They said he was extraordinary. He gave away lots of packages he was getting, of clothes and food, to people who were really suffering.' "

shadow, was gone.[48] His brother's grim fate can be glimpsed behind many pages of his novels. For literature, which can be indifferent to what brings it into being, guilt is an ideal impetus—the *perpetuum mobile* among motivations. Without the gnawing, unquenchable need for justification, certain works of literature probably never would have been written. To Nabokov's work Sergei's death imparted some moderation and ambivalence. *Ada* would be an old man's erotic dream without Ada's neglected younger sister, Lucette, who resembles the author's brother in many respects. Without Sergei, Charles Kinbote—who is musical, religious, and fond of German culture as well as young men—would have only comic sides and not also a tragic one. Though his brother's death did not tear out Nabokov's deep-seated homophobia by its roots, it added something else to the mix.

Even during Sergei's lifetime, it was not completely unmixed. Nabokov had already thought about his unhappy relationship with his brother at an earlier point in time. His novel with the saint of homosexuals in its title testifies to that. Along with the brother, this novel is devoted to a no less tormenting figure, an irresistible *dame sans merci*.

---

48  As Field relates, in a conversation with a student Nabokov immediately changed the subject when the topic of brothers came up and made it "crystal clear" that he didn't want to discuss this. (See Field, *Life and Art*, 231.)

# 4

# SEBASTIAN KNIGHT AND THE
# PERSIAN PRINCESS

Nabokov wrote his first English-language novel, *The Real Life of Sebastian Knight*, in France in 1938. To describe the conditions under which it was written as harsh would be putting it mildly. Never again in his life was Nabokov so close to despair. An attack of psoriasis caused him such intense torments that he wrote to Véra that only she and their child kept him from suicide. Meanwhile he faced the inner torment of two equally difficult decisions: he had to choose between two languages and he had to forsake one of the two women he loved. In both cases Nabokov—like Thomas Mann[1]—chose differently in life than in literature. From that point on Nabokov wrote in English. The fictitious author Sebastian Knight composes his last letter in Russian. Nabokov left his lover and stayed with his wife, Véra. His hero Sebastian leaves Clare Bishop—whose initials, read in Cyrillic and backward, reveal her source[2]—and falls in love with a woman named Nina, which rhymes with Irina, the name of the woman with whom Nabokov had a passionate affair in the spring of 1937 in Paris, the lover he had to uproot from his heart to save his marriage.[3]

---

1  In life, young Thomas Mann chose Katia and thus conventional marriage; in litera-ture, his eternal desire strives toward the central experience of his heart in his youth, Paul Ehrenberg, and his successors.
2  As Julian W. Connolly ascertained, C. B., read in Cyrillic and backward, yields V.S.—Véra Slonim. (See Dieter E. Zimmer's afterword to *Sebastian Knight* [Rowohlt], 292.)
3  Irina Guadanini was the name of the Russian émigré whom Nabokov thought he couldn't live without. His wife denied her husband's one significant affair until Brian

Both decisions weighed heavily on his heart, and they would have been enough to paralyze another man. But on top of these troubles came the hardest ordeal of all: his mother lay dying in Czechoslovakia, and he

---

Boyd informed her that Nabokov's correspondence with his lover had survived. From Stacy Schiff we learn somewhat more about this passion, which brought Nabokov to the brink of madness in 1937. (At its peak he wrote his paean to marital fidelity in *The Gift*.) Apparently Véra suspected what was keeping Vladimir in Paris in the spring of 1937, which was one reason she had been pressing him to come to her in Prague. For all the details Schiff is able to add to Boyd's version, the biographers agree on one thing: both date the start of the affair to February 1937. But it is precisely this date that confronts us with a conundrum. As Boyd and Schiff know, though Irina vanishes from Nabokov's life after the end of the affair in the summer of 1937, she does not vanish from his work, in which he plays through all the variations of what might have happened. In the 1943 epistolary story "That in Aleppo Once ..." he atones by placing himself in the position of the betrayed spouse suffering from jealousy—in a letter in which the most important line is the most inconspicuous, the salutation: "Dear V." In *Sebastian Knight* he dedicates half a novel to Irina. And it is just as hard for Nabokov as it is for his fictitious protagonist to understand the "amazing fact that a man writing of things which he really felt at the time of writing, could have had the power to create simultaneously—and out of the very things which distressed his mind—a fictitious and faintly absurd character." (*Sebastian Knight*, 114.) Nina Lecerf is the erotically irresistible angel of death, the first of those femmes fatales under whose spell the good Timofey Pnin will ultimately fall as well. But the conundrum is that she is not in fact the first. The seductive Nina with whom a married man falls in love appeared before. She surfaces in "Spring in Fialta," in which the narrator, Victor, becomes aware of his love for the alluring Nina at a point in time when fate has already decreed that it is not to be; Nina dies in an accident after he confesses his love to her. This Nina already wholly exemplifies the type of her successors: the same flighty, deceitful soul, the same erotic promiscuity, the same idiosyncrasy of resting her eyes on the lower part of the narrator's face. But this is precisely what she should not do, if she doesn't want to plunge interpreters into perplexity. For if the later Nina is derived from Irina Guadanini, then what was with the earlier one? Either Nabokov foresaw what would happen to him the following year or, more likely, the dates are wrong and the flame of the Irina affair had burned even longer than has been handed down to posterity. A few details testify in favor of this second version. Nabokov wrote "Spring in Fialta" in April 1936, immediately after the Paris trip on which he, as both biographers indicate, met Irina. Victor has his last reunion with Nina in Paris, where she is introduced to him in a salon—as Vladimir had just been to Irina. Nina's Russian fiancé is a "successful if somewhat lonesome engineer in a most distant tropical country." (*Stories*, 415.) Irina was divorced from her Russian husband, who worked in the Congo—somewhat lonesome, for Irina had no more followed him than Nina did her tropical engineer. If these parallels were a coincidence, then this was a coincidence that must have confirmed Nabokov in his tendency to see art as the dream interpreter of life.

could not visit her or even attend her funeral—a nightmare that Nabokov transposes into the final chapter of his novel, in which the narrator is hindered by endless obstacles from arriving in time at the deathbed of the person he loves most.

In those years, all refugees stood face-to-face with death, and no author could know whether his most recent project would be his final testament. By some miracle Nabokov managed not only to withstand this pressure, but also to redirect it into his art. Even among his own works there are few that so densely compress so many themes as does *The Real Life of Sebastian Knight*—only the innocent *Pnin* rivals it in this respect.

## The Invisible Man

*Sebastian Knight* contains half a dozen books in one. It's a portrait of an artist that not only makes claims about its protagonist's art, but also presents it. It's a pseudo-biography and a parody of a detective story. It's a sort of chess match, composed of knight moves, queen sacrifices, and bishops slain along the way.[4] It's a meditation on the compulsion of the past, on eros and agape, on a son's love for his mother, and on failed brotherhood. Even the theme of *The Enchanter*, the precursor to *Lolita* that Nabokov wrote in late 1939, appears in a brief flash—on his deathbed, the hero of Sebastian's last novel regrets not having spoken to an "errant schoolgirl with shameless eyes, met one day in a lonely glade."[5]

---

4   It's not for nothing that Clare's husband is named Bishop. Two bishops can be unpleasant in the endgame—that is why it's rare that both make it to that point. After touching, V. cannot take anything back: the touch-move rule. V. moves the Knight to the Bishop, the Knight slays the two Bishops, as any chess player would have done, and Clare has to go back in the box—Nabokov invites this interpretation with so many details, down to Knight's end at St. Damier, that one can understand Edmund Wilson's inclination to read the whole novel as a chess game. Above all, it is in the execution of the main intrigue that *Knight* has the character of the chess piece by that name, which cannot proceed in a straight line toward its destination, but must veer to the side. And finally, the resolution of the intrigue resembles the advance of the minor figure that transforms into the queen upon reaching the last row, the *dame sans merci* whom V. escapes by a hairsbreadth.

5   *Sebastian Knight*, 176.

A similarly intimate theme is already suggested by the title. When Sergei converted, Nabokov wrote in a letter that the mere mention of Catholicism conjured in his mind the depictions of the suffering Saint Sebastian.[6] The fact that the nude saint pierced with arrows had also always been a homosexual icon gave the name a double potency.

It's not hard to see another brotherly relationship reflected in that of the narrator to his half-brother, Sebastian. Nabokov appears to be slipping into Sergei's shoes and imagining how arrogant and remote he must have seemed to his younger brother—a bit like the conjuror Shock from "The Potato Elf." Sergei might have recognized the somewhat awkward atmosphere during the brothers' meeting in Paris as well as the scene from their youth in which the narrator gains access to Sebastian's private papers. Indeed, this book consists of snitching from the first page onward.[7] Nor would the allusions to homophilia, to Proust, and to Shakespeare's *Twelfth Night* with its male-male enamorment, have escaped the novelist's brother. According to the German Romantic writer Jean Paul, novels are only long letters to our friends, and *Sebastian Knight* contains three or four rather private ones.

And Nabokov's brother was not the only intended recipient. The narrator himself reveals to us that another letter is "a kind of code in which [Sebastian] expressed a few truths about his relations with [his wife] Clare."[8] It is the letter of separation that Nabokov could have written the previous summer to Véra and that he now incorporates into his art.

It is precisely this act—the mirroring of life in fiction—that is the major theme of *Sebastian Knight*. In a subtle fashion, Nabokov shows us that there is always a blind spot in the center of the mirror. In one of the miniatures that were so important to him he lists the books on Sebastian's shelves. There are fifteen of them; the eighth, central one is H. G. Wells's

---

6   See Schiff, *Véra*, 99.

7   Unlike his study on Gogol, which Nabokov begins with his subject's death, *The Real Life of Sebastian Knight* begins properly with his birth. It occurs on a fine, windless morning, as the narrator learns from the diary of a woman who keeps a daily record of the St. Petersburg weather and wishes to remain nameless. Then, half a page later, the narrator reveals her name after all.

8   *Sebastian Knight*, 114.

*The Invisible Man.* The title applies not only to Sebastian Knight, whose life is refracted into a thousand fictions, but also to the narrator. From the beginning to the end, we don't know whether he is Sebastian's invention or vice versa.

As for the mirroring of life in art, there is also a less-friendly version: we could also speak of a distorting mirror or of the fact that literature deceives about life. In life the truth actually looked entirely different than it did in the novel. It was not Irina who cruelly left her lover; it was Vladimir who broke off the relationship, and Irina never got over it. The novel turns the ex-lover into a vampiric creature of the race of the Lamiae, who attract men in order to suck their blood: "She sucked me dry, and in more ways than one," her first victim says.[9] Whether that was gallant of Nabokov, who later demanded back his love letters and declared that they had all been fiction, is one question. Another is the question of the truth of the novel. This truth lies in the art with which Nabokov transmutes a private passion into a deep, deep mystery play.

## Deadly Sniffle

As so often in Nabokov's work, the depths are hidden on the surface of the plot. What is it about? In search of traces of his late half-brother's life—a search that ultimately, as in Proust, constitutes the novel itself—the narrator, V., who is writing Sebastian's biography, tracks down the two women who were able to win the shy and difficult writer's heart. Who this V. really is constitutes the great riddle of the novel.[10] First he seeks out

---

9  Ibid., 145.

10  Who is this narrator and what does the V. stand for? We never find out—and not because the occasion never arises, but rather despite the fact that it presents itself repeatedly. Nabokov practically seeks out those situations in which the narrator has to introduce himself—and then he says, "I mentioned my name," instead of mentioning it. To the question of what the V. stands for—whether it is the first thing that comes to mind—Nabokov answered that it stands for Victor, which only sends the question into another loop, because "Viktor" was a private joke-name that Vladimir occasionally gave himself. (See *Selected Letters*, 21–22.) Privately, the *V* was a holy cipher between him and Véra. In *Sebastian Knight* it appears in the story of Sebastian's first love and the V-shaped flight of the cranes. (*Sebastian Knight*, 139.) But above all it marks a key scene

Clare Bishop. After the separation she avoided contact with Sebastian. The narrator visits her new apartment, where Clare lives with her second husband, who is coincidentally also named Bishop. But Mr. Bishop refuses to let V. enter: his wife wants no more contact with the past. For the sake of his work, V. persists. Two days later he attempts to accost Clare on the street and ask her about Sebastian. As he approaches her, he notices at the last moment that she is in an advanced stage of pregnancy and that he couldn't possibly bother her. But he has already crossed to her side of the street and put on a smile—there's no going back. He nearly bumps into her, and they both stop short. Now V. displays great presence of

---

shortly before the ending. At a decisive moment, when V. receives a telegram about the hopeless state of his brother, he goes "for some reason unknown"—thus an important one—into the bathroom and stands there for a moment in front of the mirror. The telegram transcribed the Russian spelling of Sebastian's name into "Se*v*astian," and this *v* seems to give our V. something to think about—probably that's where his initial comes from. Does he no longer recognize himself in the mirror, like the narrator in "Terror"? Who is real here, who fictitious? Both characters are fictional, of course, like Kinbote and Shade, but we can nonetheless wonder who is supposed to have invented whom. Brian Boyd is not the only one to have advanced the thesis that the writer Sebastian Knight dreams up the narrator V. and reveals this to the reader by having V. reenact parts of his novels. Indeed, there are many such subtle links between these novels and the plot of *Sebastian Knight*. Sebastian's name, however, seems to weaken the thesis: it is too expressive and allegorical to pass for real. Ultimately the question of reality is dissolved in the final, metaphysical twist. As for Kinbote and Shade, who have provoked the exact same debate: if everything blurs, perhaps we must cling to two striking, essential details. First of all, both characters have the same birthday (July 5), which seems to suggest a secret identity, as Carolyn Kunin on NABOKV-L was the first to propose. If it were a coincidence, this shared birthday would be a "statistical monster" similar to the chances of Kinbote's Zemblan vest pocket edition of *Timon of Athens* containing the source for the title *Pale Fire*. (See *Pale Fire*, 285.) Second, Kinbote falls out of the fiction at the end. The scenery collapses as in *Invitation to a Beheading*—or, indeed, *Sebastian Knight*. The conclusion of the latter can also apply to *Pale Fire*: He and I are identical; all individuation is illusion.

A still bolder thesis regarding the question of the "true" editor of *Pale Fire* has not yet found its way into the public discussion: the editor is Shade's wife, Sybil. Shade died of a second heart attack and was not shot, as the epigraph from Boswell already hints ("no, no, Hodge shall not be shot"). His wife consoles herself for the loss by continuing the poetic work of her beloved husband, "keeping John alive by making new the Zembla that he had made for her"—a solution that, perhaps more than any other, would have pleased Vladimir and Véra. (Private communication from the former Harvard librarian Edwin E. Williams, May 14, 2004.)

mind. He pulls out of his pocket the first thing he finds, holds it up to nearsighted Clare, and asks if she dropped it. She looks at him briefly, says "no" with an impersonal smile, and continues on her way.

Two chapters later we learn what fate awaits her: "She had seemed to be such a normal and healthy young woman, how was it that she bled to death next to an empty cradle?"[11] Yes, how was it? The narrator asks the question as one does in real life, without hope of an answer. But that's not the case for his author, who silently provides the answer through a thematic thread. The healthy young woman had met Sebastian's half-brother once before, twelve years earlier in Paris. On that occasion, V. recalls, she was hoarse and had a bad cold. Now, twelve years later, he remembers the Paris encounter due to a coincidence: Mr. Bishop, the new husband who won't let him in to see Clare, also happens to be suffering from a severe cold. The nonsensical thought flashes through V.'s mind that Mr. Bishop might have caught his cold from the red-nosed, sniffling Clare Bishop V. saw twelve years ago in Paris.

Aha! Droplet infection from the distant past—that would prefigure the answer to the question of why poor Clare had to die. The object that V. nimbly fishes out of his pocket when he can no longer avoid the pregnant woman comes from the very past from which Clare seeks in vain to protect herself. It is the key to Sebastian Knight's apartment. It is pivotal that Clare does not just look at it. It gives V. a painful pang to realize "that she had touched it with her innocent blind fingers …"

Even without the ellipsis with which the sentence and the chapter end, one senses that what is taking place here is a magical compulsion. A touch suffices, and the past bites like a snake. Like a sniffle that can still be caught more than a decade later, the past remains virulent. V. puts the key into innocent Clare's hand, and the deadly contact has been made. Clare dies in childbirth because her former lover drags her down with him into the grave. It is the magic of the fairy tale that determines the events of the novel, and it is pitch-black.

---

11  *Sebastian Knight*, 101.

## Nina's Weakness for Lhassa

Clare's successor Nina candidly acknowledges possessing a trait that is also fairy-tale-like and magical: in her presence all flowers wither. There was once a Persian princess like her, she tells V., who blighted the Palace Gardens.[12] And flowers are not the only things that fade at Nina's touch: her house is decaying prematurely, and even the blond hair of her Russian servant displays a conspicuous gray streak. Her alias, Madame Lecerf, itself makes Nina a mythological creature. She bears this name, which means "stag," not only because she gives all men cuckold's horns and because the masculine *le cerf* makes her flicker androgynously; *le cerf* also transforms the—unusually pale—woman into the white stag of the knightly epics collected in *La morte d'Arthur* on Sebastian's bookshelf. The white stag is

---

12   Ibid., 166. Nathaniel Hawthorne's "Rappaccini's Daughter" has been suggested as a possible source for this poisonous princess who blights her gardens. (See Márta Pellérdi, "Nabokov's *The Real Life of Sebastian Knight* or, What You Will.") John Keats is another source from which the motif might be drawn. As his letters and his commentary to *Eugene Onegin* show, Nabokov had the work of the English Romantic, one of his favorite poets, very much in mind. Humbert Humbert knows Keats so well that he can expatiate in an essay on the Proustian theme in a letter from the poet. It's also Humbert who remarks of his nymph that she has him "in thrall"—echoing Keats's poem of deadly eros: "La belle dame sans merci / Thee hath in thrall!" (See *The Annotated Lolita*, 183, 400.) In the first line of this poem Humbert's forerunner Sebastian would come across a name he knows well: "O what can ail thee, knight-at-arms." Not only "would"—in fact, he must have come across it: a translation of "La Belle Dame Sans Merci" is the acclaimed work of his first teacher and the first literary title mentioned in *Sebastian Knight*. Nabokov, who had himself translated "La Belle Dame" into Russian, thereby signals the direction of the plot that will drive his Knight into the arms of a fatal but irresistible lover. The companion poem of "La Belle Dame" is Keats's masterpiece "Lamia." Like "La Belle Dame" it is about a demonic woman with elfin blood who ruins a man. Lamia is a serpent. In an astonishing scene of transformation, she sheds her skin and takes on womanly form. She seduces a Corinthian and lives with him in a palace. On their wedding day, she cringes under the piercing gaze of a philosopher. After his cry "A Serpent!" she vanishes into thin air. As her spell is being broken, a thousand myrtle wreaths wilt in the palace, a motif from her initial transformation, during which the foam from Lamia's mouth makes the grass wither. In her human form Lamia is a Persian, a divergence from the Greek myth in which she was a Phoenician. All this, along with the leitmotif "pale," the ice-cold hand, the sapphires of the snakeskin, Nabokov might have plucked from Keats and attached to Sebastian's witch.

the strange and wondrous animal that lures the hunting knight into the cave of love.

Pregnant Clare is not the only one subject to an evil compulsion; so too is Sebastian Knight when he follows Nina into this cave of love. And he, too, is under the spell of the past. Nina is a revenant of his flighty mother, Virginia, who died young. The gift that Virginia, who lived apart from his father, gave to her son on her only visit and that he preserves as a keepsake, a small parcel of sugar-coated violets, reappears to him in Nina, who wears violet eye shadow. Sebastian can no more break free from his dead mother than he can resist Nina. He follows his mother when he plunges into the misery of his last love. But his *belle dame sans merci* has more than unhappiness in store for him. Indeed, this sorrow has abysses that no disciple may shun.

Nina Lecerf, mythologically charged and yet as vivid as only few Nabokov characters, teaches Sebastian a lesson that helps him achieve the finale of his last novel. The Russian woman with the animal in her name knows more about death than others do. It's no accident that she is reminiscent of Madame Chauchat in this respect. "*Le corps, l'amour, la mort, ces trois ne font qu'un,*" Hans Castorp learned from his Russian beloved in *The Magic Mountain.*[13] In the cave of the Blauberg hotel the author of *The Funny Mountain* learns how love, death, and art intertwine. Madame Lecerf is the muse of his last novel. What this muse reveals to him is the secret of unity.

In a way it is the secret of the whole novel. Why do the many books compressed into *Sebastian Knight* not break into disconnected fragments? The answer is already concealed in the title. A knight wears armor. Sebastian is the nude martyr pierced by arrows. The components of the name are mutually exclusive. Indeed, it is impossible that an armored book of fiction—which is what *Sebastian Knight* undoubtedly is—can portray something like naked *Real Life*. Either Sebastian or Knight: either real life or fiction. A book with this contradictory title apparently seeks to

---

13  Mann, *The Magic Mountain*, 407. In the edition cited, the phrase—in French in the original—is translated into English as "*The body, love, death, are simply one and the same.*" (Italics in original.)

deal with the "either" *and* the "or," the *coincidentia oppositorum*, to use an expression from medieval theology: the coincidence of opposites.

It is not a contradiction that the novel shows us this principle almost exclusively *ex negativo*—as if it were the hidden God, who reveals himself only once in an eon. On the contrary, that is the point of the novel. Only at the climaxes of *Sebastian Knight* do we witness how opposites merge into a higher unity. Most of the time things scatter in all directions. There's not one chapter in this book in which something is not mixed up, lost, forgotten, or mistaken. Sebastian anticipates the last and most dramatic of these mix-ups in an autobiographical novel: the mother of this novel's protagonist dies in a French pension called "Les Violettes." By chance, her son ends up in the area and finds the pension with a bunch of violets painted on the gate. There he has a brief vision of his mother in the empty garden. After his return to England, he learns that his mother died in a place of the same name in an entirely different part of France.

The narrator who quotes the passage should have taken it as a warning. In the last chapter, with much luck, he makes it in time to the hospital where his brother Sebastian lies dying. He gives his name and is permitted to stay. V. sits outside the sickroom and, listening to his brother breathing, experiences a sort of mystical communion and consolation. But then he learns that the names have been mixed up; Sebastian has already died, and he has been sitting outside the door of a complete stranger.

The paths that lead the narrator to his discovery of Nina are also winding. A Frenchwoman tells him about her friend, a Russian woman, for two chapters. From her description it becomes evident that the Russian woman must be Nina, Sebastian's last lover, whom V. is seeking. Soon she will arrive and emerge from the fog. Just as V. is about to while away the wait by embarking on a little adventure with the not unattractive friend, a tiny detail makes him suspicious. To test his hunch, he mutters to the servant in Russian: "I think there is a spider on the nape of her neck." The hand of the supposed Frenchwoman flies up to her neck, and the end of the chapter—the climax of one of the most elegant intrigues in Nabokov's work—reveals the truth: the friend herself is the Russian Nina whom V. is seeking; she has been speaking of herself in the third person the whole time. In a stunning effect, two characters merge into one.[14]

The trick is always the same: A turns out to be B; the apparently insignificant minor character is unmasked as the main character. Nabokov gives a philosophical dimension to the narrative feint that he had occasion to study in Chesterton's work.[15] The point of all the mix-ups is their resolution. For a mix-up, two things are required, but "the only real number is one," writes Sebastian, "the rest are mere repetition."[16]

*Tat tvam asi*, a Hindu dictum meaning "you are that," is not unknown to the belatedly exposed Nina Lecerf: "She had a weakness for Lhassa," explains her first, depleted husband, "you know what I mean …"[17] The

---

14   The following events lead up to the final combination: 1. V. visits one of the addresses that are wondrously provided to him and meets two chess-playing Russians and a child. From the father's story about his first wife he is able to deduce that she could be Sebastian's last lover. 2. The child with the chess-playing men is bored and begins to draw. 3. The child's uncle (who beats the father in chess) draws him a racing car with incredible rapidity. 4. Out of embarrassment, the narrator says that he, the uncle, is an artist. 5. The father overhears from the kitchen and says his cousin is an all-around genius, can play the violin standing on his head, multiply one telephone number by another in three seconds, and write his name upside down in his ordinary handwriting. 6. At his next address V. meets a French friend of a Russian woman who is out of town at the moment. What the Frenchwoman tells him about her absent friend sounds very much like Sebastian's last lover. 7. The Russian woman arrives at her friend's house. The narrator does not set eyes on her right away. While he is waiting, he sits on a garden bench next to the Frenchwoman, whom he begins to find attractive. Embarrassed once again, he draws lines on the ground with a stick. She asks what he's trying to draw, and he answers, "My thought-waves." "Once upon a time," she says softly, "I kissed a man just because he could write his name upside down." The penny drops, the narrator comprehends and performs the test with the Russian sentence. The minor character transforms into the main character. It shouldn't surprise us if the shrewd cousin had also had a relationship with Madame Lecerf and was the true father of the child to whom he is so attentive. It is the spider's web of such microplots below the surface of the main plot that keeps Nabokov's work from getting old.

15   Many Father Brown stories end with two apparently separate characters becoming identical. For Nabokov and Chesterton, see Maar, "Everlasting Men," in *Die falsche Madeleine*, 114–28, and David Rampton, "Nabokov and Chesterton," in *Nabokov Studies* 8 (2004), 43–57.

16   *Sebastian Knight*, 105, 113. It is the only phrase in the book that Nabokov repeats.

17   Ibid., 147.

resolution of the mix-up is the moment in Sebastian's late work when the self is about to unveil the ultimate, dazzling, all-embracing truth. Unfortunately, we don't find out what it is, because this self dies just in time, but we witness its effect: the brain breaks out of the "iron ring" that encompasses it, the "close-fitting dream of one's own personality."[18] All individuation is merely the deception of Maya, a dream from which the novel awakes with the last sentence: "I am Sebastian, or Sebastian is I, or perhaps we both are someone whom neither of us knows."[19]

That not only sounds like a hard nut for interpreters to crack, dividing them once again into numerous schools. It also sounds much like a thinker who often seems to meander through Nabokov's work.

---

18   Ibid., 179.
19   Ibid., 205. So does Sebastian live on in V. or in the unknown third party? In the final passage of "Hyperion" Keats expresses the paradox "to die into life." It refers to the birth of art. That is how Nabokov's protagonist dies as well, into real life, into *The Real Life of Sebastian Knight*.

# 5

# Ultima Thule

*And see, no longer blinded by our eyes*
(Rupert Brooke)

Someone should run an iron over the questionnaire that Nabokov filled out in 1971, to find out whether a name is inscribed in invisible ink where there is such a gaping blank. All the literary questions he answers in detail, but under "works of philosophy" there is—nothing. Did he never pick up a philosophical work? If so, he certainly didn't publicize the fact. Aside from a strong aversion to Plato, not much is known about his judgments. Privately, he cited another thinker at a significant moment. The same year in which he presented himself as philosophically abstinent he took a mountain hike with his son—it would be the last they would share—and looked back on his successful life. On that occasion, he told Dmitri that he had accomplished what he wished in his work. From the beginning, he went on, "his writing was all there, ready inside his mind, like film waiting to be developed. A sensation, he said, akin to Schopenhauer's vision of events as they unfold."[1]

Nabokov shared more with the author of *The World as Will and Representation* than puzzled surprise that we view the dark eternity before our

---

1   Boyd, *The American Years*, 585. That one little sentence reverberates as far-reachingly as Thomas Mann's casual confession in his old age that "The Steadfast Tin Soldier" was the fundamental symbol of his life. Nabokov usually weighed his words. In order to see his life reflected in a category or a vision of Schopenhauer, he must have felt closer to him than the questionnaires and offical interviews reveal.

birth with more calm than the one after our death.[2] He had deep affinities with Schopenhauer, who saw himself as the Kaspar Hauser of philosophy. One of them was that the thinker did not regard art and philosophy as antagonistic sisters, but rather as Siamese twins. If there was ever a philosopher for artists, it was Arthur Schopenhauer. Another appeal of his thought was all that he suggested about the great secret: death and the unity behind individuation.

"I do not know if it has ever been noted before," writes the narrator of *Pnin*, "that one of the main characteristics of life is discreteness. Unless a film of flesh envelops us, we die … The cranium is a space-traveler's helmet. Stay inside or you perish. Death is divestment, death is communion. It may be wonderful to mix with the landscape, but to do so is the end of the tender ego."[3] Nabokov knew well that it had been noted before and that he was only creating new metaphors for Schopenhauer's old *principium individuationis*. Nabokov's imagery is even sharper: not a veil being lifted, but a helmet bursting. That doesn't change the result. The negation of the principle of individuation leads, as in the last sentence of

---

2   In the chapter "On Death and Its Relation to the Indestructibility of Our Inner Nature," Schopenhauer writes: "If what makes death seem so terrible to us were the thought of *non-existence*, we should necessarily think with equal horror of the time when as yet we did not exist. For it is irrefutably certain that non-existence after death cannot be different from non-existence before birth, and is therefore no more deplorable than that is. An entire infinity ran its course when we did *not yet* exist, but this in no way disturbs us. On the other hand, we find it hard, and even unendurable, that after the momentary intermezzo of an ephemeral existence, a second infinity should follow in which we shall exist *no longer*." (*The World as Will and Representation*, vol. II, 466.) The passage reads like a draft of the famous first page of Nabokov's autobiography, which expands on the very same idea: "The cradle rocks above an abyss, and common sense tells us that our existence is but a brief crack of light between two eternities of darkness. Although the two are identical twins, man, as a rule, views the prenatal abyss with more calm than the one he is heading for (at some forty-five hundred heartbeats an hour). I know, however, of a young chronophobiac who experienced something like panic when looking for the first time at homemade movies that had been taken a few weeks before his birth"—panic that increases at the sight of a new baby carriage that is empty like a coffin, "as if, in the reverse course of events, his very bones had disintegrated." (*Speak, Memory*, 19.)
3   *Pnin*, 20.

*Sebastian Knight*, to the confluence of an "I" with a "he." The passage in the novel before this final unveiling is already pure Schopenhauer—the actors on stage playing their roles, the hereafter as the abolition of individuation, "the full ability of consciously living in any chosen soul, in any number of souls." Once one has broken out of the iron ring of individuation, the world discloses its meaning, as it is revealed to Sebastian's dying character: "Now the puzzle was solved."[4]

According to Schopenhauer, it was not only philosophy but also art that strove for the solution to this puzzle.[5] But could it really be solved? Schopenhauer had his doubts: "[T]he actual, positive solution to the riddle of the world must be something that the human intellect is wholly incapable of grasping and conceiving; so that if a being of a higher order came and took all the trouble to impart it to us, we should be quite unable to understand any part of his disclosures."[6]

Nabokov gives this thought a demonic turn as well: not only would we not understand his disclosures, they would kill us. In the first chapter of the unfinished novel *Solus Rex*, titled "Ultima Thule," he introduces Adam Falter, who has a "diabolical dialogue" with the narrator about ultimate truth.[7] The narrator has just lost his wife and seeks consolation from the man, who is either a charlatan or the being that Schopenhauer had in mind.

One night after a visit to a bordello, Adam Falter was struck by lightning—not ordinary lightning, but "unearthly lightning," a flash of knowledge that made him howl for five minutes without interruption like a woman in childbirth with "a giant in her womb." Falter survives and is

---

4   *Sebastian Knight*, 204, 179.

5   "Not merely philosophy but also the fine arts work at bottom towards the solution of the problem of existence. For in every mind which once gives itself up to the purely objective contemplation of the world, a desire has been awakened, however concealed and unconscious, to comprehend the true nature of things, of life, and of existence." (*The World as Will and Representation*, vol. II, 406.)

6   Ibid., vol. II, 185.

7   *Stories*, 522. The very name Falter hints at the theme of metamorphosis in death, as depicted in the story "Christmas." See also *Selected Letters*, 413 (*Falter* is a German word for butterfly).

transformed into a monster. By all appearances, he has gone insane, but he claims to stand "outside our world, in the true reality." The first person he allows to elicit from him one word too many about absolute truth dies immediately of heart failure. Thereafter, Falter restrains himself. To the narrator's grilling he responds: "I cannot explain it to you, since the least hint of an explanation would be a lethal glimpse." When Falter is dying, he sends the narrator a final letter. He writes that he "would die on Tuesday, and that in parting he ventured to inform me that—here followed two lines which had been painstakingly and, it seemed, ironically blacked out."[8]

Even if we had infrared light this time instead of an iron, we would of course find nothing there. The pattern is always the same and necessarily paradoxical. Sebastian Knight's protagonist dies a second before he can put the all-revealing sentence down on paper. Timofey Pnin is on the verge of the great explanation of the universe when he's interrupted by a thirsty rodent. Adam Falter, however, inadvertently gave himself away, as he confesses to the narrator: in all his talk, two or three words were hidden in which flashed a "fringe of absolute insight."[9] Is he just blowing his own horn? What could those words possibly be? Nabokov hid them carefully. Adam Falter refers to something that he could scarcely have known. He is aware of private penchants of the narrator's late wife about which he could not have been informed.[10] Nabokov thereby shows that he did not intend Falter, who also correctly predicts the date of his own death, to be a fraud. And he feeds the suspicion all the more that the same could be true of Sebastian Knight's late work.

Sometimes, when he turns the pages of Sebastian's masterpiece, V. tells us, he feels that:

---

8   *Stories*, 506, 500, 513, 522.

9   Ibid., 522.

10   There are three things the narrator's late wife likes most in life: verse, wildflowers, and foreign currency. Falter alludes to this, which he would not be able to do as a mere charlatan. (See Ibid., 510, 515, and D. Barton Johnson, "Nabokov as Gnostic Seeker," in *Worlds in Regression*, 208, 214.)

the "absolute solution" is there, somewhere, concealed in some passage I have read too hastily, or that it is intertwined with other words whose familiar guise deceived me. I don't know any other book that gives one this special sensation, and perhaps this was the author's special intention.[11]

It is even quite certain that this was the author's special intention. Time and again Nabokov's reader feels that there, somewhere between the lines, the great truth is hidden. It has rolled under the sofa, and if we could only extend our fingertips a little bit farther, we would have it in our hands. And the second feeling that creeps up on the reader time and again is this: Nabokov, like Falter, wasn't bluffing.

Isaiah Berlin makes a famous distinction between two types of authors: the fox and the hedgehog. The fox knows many things, but the hedgehog knows one big thing. Tolstoy, he argues, was actually a fox who forced himself to be a hedgehog. Was Nabokov a hedgehog who knew one big thing that could not be expressed other than in the medium of art?

## The Shimmer Behind the Horror

Among the thinkers of the nineteenth century, Arthur Schopenhauer is regarded as one of the most mystical. Nabokov is not the least so among the writers of the twentieth. His oft-quoted statement "I know more than I can express in words, and the little I can express would not have been expressed, had I not known more"[12]—this sentence released into the world by *Playboy* is the fundamental formula of every mysticism of art and the artist that wants to lure into language what lies beyond it.

In a posthumously published note, Schopenhauer writes:

> Perhaps we shudder before death mainly because it represents the darkness from which we once emerged and into which we shall now return. But I believe that when death closes our eyes, we will stand in a light of which our sunlight is but the shadow.[13]

---

11  *Sebastian Knight*, 180.
12  *Strong Opinions*, 45. It is one of Nabokov's sentences that we know will survive.
13  See Arthur Schopenhauer, *Der handschriftliche Nachlaß III*, 523 (trans. Ross Benjamin).

Though Nabokov left no such note, his whole oeuvre indicates that he shared Schopenhauer's belief—even if this belief was persistently undermined. The bizarre Adam Falter, who seems to hold the great solution in his hand, is followed by the poet Shade, who believes he sees the proof of immortality in black and white before his eyes. During a heart attack that brings him to the brink of death, a tall white fountain appears to him. Shortly thereafter he reads in a magazine about a Mrs. Z., who reports exactly the same vision from her near-death experience: In "The Land Beyond the Veil" she "glimpsed a tall white fountain." Shade's conclusion seems logical:

> If on some nameless island Captain Schmidt
> Sees a new animal and captures it,
> And if, a little later, Captain Smith
> Brings back a skin, that island is no myth.

To dispel his remaining doubts, Shade obtains Mrs. Z.'s address from the author of the article. But the visit comes to nothing, and he has to escape before Mrs. Z., who turns out to be an admirer of his poems, attempts to unite her soul all too intimately with his own. The journalist, whom he meets again, assures him he has not changed her notes. Only one misprint crept in, quite minor: "*Mountain*, not *fountain*."[14]

"Life Everlasting—based on a misprint!" Shade's hope is dashed, and must be built up again only gradually. Like the medusa experience, Nabokov's metaphysics is not rigid, but rather in flux.[15] But a clear-cut division reigns over this flux, a dichotomy between dark and light. The laughter in the dark stands for the evil world, in opposition to the world of light. There is, however, nothing warming or consoling about this light. It is the light of mystical knowledge and death. In "Ultima Thule" it was lightning with which absolute knowledge struck. In the story "Spring in Fialta" it is the sunlight that breaks through the cloud cover and begins to

---

14   See *Pale Fire*, 60–62, and Maar, "Everlasting Men," in *Die falsche Madeleine*, 117.

15   *Pale Fire*, 62. Priscilla Meyer rightly observes that Nabokov conducts an ongoing argument with himself. ("Dolorous Haze, Hazel Shade: Nabokov and the Spirits" in *Nabokov's World*, vol. 1, 88–103.)

shine just as the narrator becomes aware of his love and his beloved dies in a car crash. Light, love, and death merge into an enigmatic trinity. In the novel *Bend Sinister* it is a glimmer that grows increasingly strong and releases the hero from the world of his torments.

In this book Nabokov would develop an idea that had *never* been treated before, the author proclaimed solemnly before the writing of *Bend Sinister*.[16] This idea shone through in his working title for the novel, *The Person from Porlock*, an allusion to the unwelcome visitor, "a person on business from Porlock," who rudely awakened the Romantic poet Samuel Taylor Coleridge from his creative trance. Coleridge had been writing the poem "Kubla Khan" as it came to him in an opium dream, and would have gone on writing had the visitor not disturbed him and yanked him back into reality. The poem remained a fragment because Coleridge could not remember the rest of the vision after this interruption. In English literary history Porlock has been a quite infamous place ever since.

Why does *Bend Sinister* allude to Coleridge's opium dream? In Nabokov's novel, too, someone is abruptly wrenched out of his trance into another reality. The novel relates how its protagonist, Adam Krug, is repeatedly haunted by intimations that his world, a Nazi-Stalinist nightmare ruled by the dictator Paduk, is not the real world. It dawns on the character that he is only a character—or rather, a glimmer of this idea appears to him. Here, too, the distant light that Adam Krug perceives is linked to love and death in an enigmatic trinity. First Adam Krug loses his beloved wife, Olga, and then his son is mixed up with another boy and killed by sadistic youths in a sanatorium as a cathartic "release-instrument." Before Krug can fathom the agony of this loss, the author takes pity on him and plunges him into insanity.[17] In the last scene the deranged Krug is shot by Paduk's bodyguard. At the moment of his death, the author breaks off the charade, stands up from his desk, and investigates what has been rattling against the wire netting of his window (a moth,

---

16    See *Dear Bunny, Dear Volodya*, 136.
17    See *Bend Sinister*, 233.

which had also fluttered through Adam Krug's world as the emblem for Olga's soul).

It is he, the inventor of fictional worlds, who is the person from Porlock. Unlike in the Coleridge incident, he doesn't appear as a disturber but rather as a redeemer. In a sense, the creator takes his Adam to his paternal bosom, snatching him out of an intolerable world into another— but which? Adam has a vague suspicion all along that beyond the horizon lies a hidden realm of which he can perceive strange outlines and traces of light as if through frosted glass—that is the crux of the novel. Nabokov embeds the idea in the narrative structure itself. That is what is uniquely new about his idea, as he explains in a letter: to let the character slowly realize that the author created him and watches over him. This is, he writes, "if you like, a kind of symbol of the Divine power."[18]

And this from the well-known despiser of all symbols! Apparently there is something that Nabokov urgently wants to express with his formal idea. As Adam is released from the fiction by the artist, so too might we other Adams be released at our appointed hour from our more densely woven dream. There's not only horror behind the shimmer. Perhaps there is also a shimmer behind the horror.

## The Vane Sisters

That's something Cynthia and Sybil Vane would know best. As with *Bend Sinister,* Nabokov announced that he had ventured something singular with the short story "The Vane Sisters." He declared in all modesty that the trick he performed in it "can be tried only once in a thousand years of fiction."[19]

---

18   *Selected Letters,* 50.
19   From his notes to "The Vane Sisters." (See *Stories,* 659.) "Nothing of this kind has ever been attempted by any author," he repeats in his congratulatory letter to the first five code-crackers in *Encounter.* (See *Selected Letters,* 286.) He was fond of stressing the singularity of his creations (and never wholly without justification). Of *Lolita* he asserts that the book "has had no precedent in literature." Regarding Professor Pnin, he announces: "What I am offering you is a character entirely new to literature." In the case of *Pale Fire* it's his wife who writes for him: "not like anything either he or anyone else has ever written before." (Ibid., 140, 178, 331.)

At first glance, the millennial character of the story doesn't leap off the page. On the surface, not much more happens in it than that a French college professor recalls his relationship with two sisters who have since died. Sybil Vane, the younger sister, committed suicide when her lover, the narrator's colleague, ended their affair. After Sybil's death—perhaps partially out of guilt because he had talked his adulterous colleague out of his infidelity—the narrator keeps in touch with her sister, Cynthia, who draws him into her spiritualist circles. Cynthia has exact ideas of how the spirits of the dead influence her life through gentle interventions. Whatever happens, whatever strange chance occurrence befalls her, Cynthia recognizes the spectral source—her world is full of signs and symbols from the afterlife.

The narrator listens to all this and even sits in on her séances, but doesn't take the eccentric Vane sister too seriously. One day he comments a bit too mockingly on her parties, at which point Cynthia berates him and he drops out of contact with her. Then one day—the day with which the story begins—he learns that Cynthia died of a heart condition. And now the rumblings begin. He lies awake at night and listens anxiously to every creak: Could it be a sign from Cynthia, who can finally prove her theories? He tries to set his mind at ease by reviewing all the cases of fraudulent mediums—he is conspicuously well versed in this subject.[20] But sleep doesn't come until dawn. The dream he then has, which he immediately searches for subtle messages, remains vague and muddled.

That is the plot. There are only two things missing from this account: the trick at the end, and the beginning without which this trick cannot be understood. Before the narrator learns of Cynthia's death, he takes a winter stroll that he describes in detail. In particular, two effects of light and shadow absorb his attention and lead to his encounter with the unfaithful husband who was to blame for the suicide of the first Vane sister and who now informs him of the death of the second. Initially, there is

---

20 In addition to "Nabokov and the Spirits," the above-cited essay by Priscilla Meyer, D. Barton Johnson's essay "Nabokov and de la Mare" deals with Nabokov's intimacy with spiritualism (*Nabokov's World*, vol. 1, 71–87).

nothing too remarkable about what seems at most a somewhat excessively meticulous description of these two light effects with which Nabokov prefaces the more eventful passages. What the narrator sees and what delights him are two plays of shadow: a dripping icicle and the red-tinged reflection of a parking meter. By the time we reach the end of the story, we have forgotten these pretty but apparently incidental details. The final paragraph, the final rumination of the awakened narrator, leaves the reader wondering as well:

> I could isolate, consciously, little. Everything seemed blurred, yellow-clouded, yielding nothing tangible. Her inept acrostics, maudlin evasions, theopathies—every recollection formed ripples of mysterious meaning. Everything seemed yellowly blurred, illusive, lost.[21]

What sort of impenetrable hocus-pocus is this? Can an author leave off his story with such frayed ends, with everything yellowly blurred and inept acrostics?

As a matter of fact, in that last word lies the hidden key to the obscure passage. So as to be fair, Nabokov placed it where it was needed. An acrostic is a poem in which the first letters of the lines or verses spell out a word or a whole sentence. Nabokov alludes to this encryption method twice in the course of the tale; with its help the narrator tries to draw secret messages from Shakespeare's sonnets. Attentive readers, at least, are not completely unprepared when they stumble on the enigmatic ending with its "yellowly." Why, of all adverbs, this one? Because a *y* is needed—to be precise, the *y* in Sybil. Scanned as an acrostic, the paragraph reads as follows: *Icicles by Cynthia. Meter from me, Sybil.*

There we have it. Apparently it's no longer the narrator speaking at the end, but someone else. Parking meter and icicle, the pretty light effects—it was the dead sisters who arranged them and nudged the narrator onto the right path. And that's not all. Not only do the sisters make shadows and red light for the narrator; with their ghostly fingers they also guide his pen. Sybil and Cynthia dictate his closing sentences,

---

21  *Stories*, 631.

which he writes without knowing what is hidden in them. He is the unsuspecting bearer of a message that he himself does not understand. It is indeed a technical trick that one cannot use every week, but perhaps only once in a thousand years.

But beyond all compositional sleights of hand: What is Nabokov up to when he conspires with the Vane sisters, just as he did with Adam Falter? And he had done it before. As early as in *Glory* he depicts someone anxiously awaiting knock codes from the beyond. Young Martin lies awake the night after the death of his father: "If, right now, a board in the floor creaks or there is a knock of some kind, that means he hears me and responds." Like the Vane sisters' friend, Martin cannot make sense of the dream that follows. Many chapters later he has a strange feeling of déjà vu: a detail from this dream, an apparently senseless sentence, suddenly becomes reality.[22] The novel remains silent as to whether Martin's departed father, who hovers as a ghost beyond the walls of time, is responsible for this glimpse into the future. Perhaps Martin, too, is a case for J. W. Dunne.

## An Experiment with Time

A large building filled with heavily rolling black smoke, a helplessly swaying water jet from a fire hose, a wooden plankway from which people are dropping in heaps, horrible choking cries, and thickening billows of black smoke—John William Dunne was thankful when he awoke from his nightmare. And yet he had been forewarned. As a child he had already had strange dreams, and as an adult he began to pay attention to them. Therefore he was not surprised the day after his dream when he

---

22 Ibid., 11–12, 177. The strange sentence in Martin's dream is: "*Gruziny ne edyat morozhenogo*": Georgians (Gruzinians) do not eat ice cream. In the forty-second chapter, Martin's acquaintance Gruzinov, in reply to an invitation, declares that he never eats ice cream. Martin, we thus find confirmed, is "that rarity—a person whose 'dreams come true.'" (*Glory*, xii.) Martin even foresees his own end in his dream of getting lost in the woods—translated into reality: getting caught on the Russian border and shot as a spy.

read the news in the evening paper. In a rubber factory near Paris, a devastating fire had broken out. The mass of smoke was so dense that it suffocated even the female workers who had escaped onto the balcony before the ladders could arrive.[23]

How could the dreamer have foreseen these exact circumstances? Clairvoyance or telepathy struck Dunne as unsatisfactory explanations. Another dream set him on the right track. In the spring of 1902, Dunne was stationed in South Africa as an officer in the Boer War. At this time he dreamed of an island that was in imminent danger of a volcanic eruption. Dunne wanted to help evacuate the four thousand inhabitants in ships. The mountain will explode, he thought in the dramatic dream, and tried in vain to rouse the inert French officials to action. When the *Daily Telegraph* arrived in his camp after the usual delay, it brought the headline of a volcano disaster in Martinique. The mountain had exploded, they had tried in vain to rescue the inhabitants in ships—all was exactly as foretold in the dream, except that the number of victims was substantially higher than the dreamed number. There were 40,000 dead, not 4,000; Dunne had been off by a zero.

What could one conclude from this? The dream seemed to be derived not from the volcanic eruption itself, but rather from the skimmed newspaper report. If Dunne had had the dream not before but after reading the newspaper, there would have been nothing unusual about it. Other dreams confirmed the pattern. The interesting thing was not that the details were accurate but that many were not accurate—while the basic situation was correctly reproduced. It couldn't be a matter of clairvoyance. The dream seemed to be composed of the day's residues, with the usual little distortions. John W. Dunne was having perfectly ordinary dreams—only he was having them on the wrong nights. They processed events that would be past only in the future.

---

23  See J. W. Dunne, *An Experiment with Time*, 44–47. In his *Annotated Lolita*, regarding a reference to "Jerome Dunn," Alfred Appel, Jr., offers a "non-note" and "anti-annotation," "which simply state that Nabokov intended no allusion whatsoever." (*The Annotated Lolita*, 334.) As laudable as the idea of the "non-note" may be, this particular case happens to be questionable.

Growing suspicious, the nocturnal prophet was determined to get to the bottom of the matter. He refused to believe he had gone mad, and decided to analyze his strange gift. Dunne rolled up his sleeves and began to investigate the true nature of time. Many concrete diagrams adorn his 1927 book *An Experiment with Time*, which presents endlessly stratified levels of time and won its author fame that has faded today. The future, he argued, was divided from the past only at our everyday level. At the higher level of so-called serial observers, the distinction no longer applies. It is not time that moves, but rather the observer. This necessitates further dimensions of time to be observed and further observers, and so on in infinite regress. In sleep or in a state of deep relaxation the human being can slide onto this higher level. The dream is a sort of porthole through which the dreamer is able to gaze upon the sea of time, which doesn't flow in one direction and which dissolves the difference between past and future in its foam.

In our everyday conscious state, however, we are so fixated on a one-way temporal flow that it requires an almost superhuman effort to turn our head in thought and relate a dream retrospectively to an event that took place at a later point in time. Only iron discipline makes such investigations possible: a diary in which the subject records all the details of his dream upon waking in order to test its hit rate in light of later occurrences. Dunne made his family and his circle of friends undertake this mental effort. In the appendix to his book he lists banal incidents and related dreams for many pages. The reader has to guess in which cases the event preceded the dream and in which cases it followed it. The answers are provided on the last page, as in a puzzle book.

Dunne wants to train our ability to make more hits—even in metaphysics the Englishman is animated by the spirit of sports. *An Experiment with Time* is perfectly sober, free of romantic enthusiasm, and not without a dry humor. And if the diagrams somewhat recall the instructions for model-making, that's no accident: Dunne was an aeronautical engineer, not a philosopher. One could spend a long time searching his index for the name Schopenhauer. And yet for a brief period he had a comparatively strong influence on the writers among his readers: James Joyce,

T. S. Eliot, and H. G. Wells had a high regard for him; Borges cited him frequently; and he even turns up in the work of Arno Schmidt.

Nabokov not only cited him and had a high regard for him—he also kept a dream diary according to Dunne's instructions.[24] In *Ada*, much of Van's philosophical treatise, *The Texture of Time*, is indebted to Dunne's second book, *The Serial Universe*. The follow-up volume—which Dunne presented to an audience of 1,500 at the London Book Fair in 1937—must have been still more important. The title already indicated where his dream theory would ultimately lead him: *The New Immortality*. In this book, the critic of Einstein and creator of Serialism provided the mathematical proof of immortality. In "real time" a rose that bloomed once blooms forever. Death is a phenomenon within the three-dimensional continuum that does not affect continued existence on the higher levels.

Nabokov had something similar in mind when he wrote—in a 1941 essay against common sense—that it was "something more than an optimistic conjecture, and even more than a matter of religious faith" that "human life is but a first installment of the serial soul and that one's individual secret is not lost in the process of earthly dissolution." He pays tribute to his intellectual forerunner by explicitly taking up his neologism (in a clever play on words).[25]

---

24   When he began the dream diary in the sixties, Nabokov used the 1934 edition of J. W. Dunne's *Experiment*. For his notes for *The Texture of Time*, incorporated into *Ada*, he consulted the 1945 edition of *The Serial Universe*. (See Marina Grishakova, "V. Nabokov's *Bend Sinister*: A Social Message or an Experiment with Time?" in *Sign Systems Studies* 28, 242–63.) Dunne's instructions required that the recording of the dream should be kept free of any interpretation. Only the details should be noted—as many as possible and especially the unusual ones. Most people first noticed retrospectively, when rereading the diary, that they had already dreamed exactly what they would later experience. And even in the process of reading, an almost insurmountable cognitive mechanism prevented them from recognizing the prophetic details that stood before their eyes in black and white. But Dunne also warned against his own method: after several days, one might concentrate while dreaming on the need to retain the dream, which could lead to insomnia. Nabokov knew a thing or two about that.

25   "The Art of Literature and Commonsense" in *Lectures on Literature*, 377.

The dreams that came true were a strong argument for Dunne's model of serial time. Nabokov may not have had enough physics to follow all the explanations, but he didn't need it. It wasn't only from Cynthia Vane's circle that he was acquainted with prophetic dreams.

# 6

# DEATH IS SWEET

He tried everything short of suicide, the Dunne reader confesses in his autobiography, to distinguish a personal glimmer in the impersonal darkness on both sides of his life. As this passage reveals, metaphysics was not an intellectual game for Nabokov, but something urgently and terribly serious. Nor was the deciphering of nocturnal messages a game. Brian Boyd relates that Nabokov had lucid dreams. After receiving the film offer that made him rich in the wake of *Lolita*'s success, he immediately recalled a dream he had had forty years earlier after the death of his uncle—the same Uncle Ruka who had fondled him and from whom he came into his first fortune, only to have it snatched from him by the Russian Revolution. He would come back to him—these were Ruka's words, which the young heir had dreamed at the time without understanding them—as "Harry and Kuvrykin." Forty years later Nabokov remembered the dream, when not his uncle but the lost fortune returned. The check for the movie rights to *Lolita* was signed by the film company of Harris and Kubrick.

The dream herald seems not to have completely mastered the English consonants. Another dream was much more distressing than this half-fulfilled one. In the fall of 1945 Nabokov dreamed of Sergei, whom he believed to be safe with Hermann at Schloss Weissenstein in Tirol. In the dream he saw him in agony in a German concentration camp. The next day came the news: Sergei had died in Neuengamme.

Another catastrophe—the fundamental catastrophe of his life—was supposedly foretold to the family by a medium.[1] On March 28, 1922, Vladimir had returned home at nine in the evening and was reading Blok's poems about Italy to his mother when the telephone rang. The old family friend Iosif Hessen stammered that something terrible had happened to Vladimir's father, and a car was coming to pick them up. The night journey with his mother struck Vladimir as something "*outside life*, monstrously slow, like those mathematical puzzles that torment us in feverish half-sleep":

> I looked at the lights swimming past, at the whitish bands of lighted pavement, at the spiral reflections in the mirrory-black asphalt, and it seemed to me that I was cut off from all this in some fateful manner—that the streetlights and the dark shadows of passersby were an accidental mirage, and the sole thing clear and significant and alive was the grief, tenacious, suffocating, compressing my heart. "Father is no more."[2]

What had happened was reported in the *Berliner Tageblatt* the next morning under the headline "Revolver Attack by Russian Monarchists in the Philharmonic":

> Yesterday evening Paul Nikolayevich Milyukov, the former Russian minister and leader of the Kadets, held a lecture at the Philharmonic on Russia's current situation and prospects for the future. When Milyukov had concluded several hours of remarks with the prospect of Russia's development into a democratic republic, he left the stage to take a break. He had invited questions from the audience, which he intended to answer after the break. The moment he left the stage to proceed out of the hall, several young men armed with revolvers forced their way to him and fired several shots at him from a distance of a few paces. These shots were accompanied by spirited but incomprehensible (probably Russian) exclamations. Milyukov collapsed immediately. Mr. Nabokov, who had formerly edited the newspaper *Rech'* with Milyukov in St. Petersburg and was, like Milyukov, among the leaders of the Kadet Party, had been standing close beside Milyukov at the moment of the assassination attempt. He leaped up to protect his friend Milyukov, was himself hit and fell

---

1  See Field, *Life and Art*, 30–31. Field suggests that Nabokov's spiritualism derived from his mother.
2  Boyd, *The Russian Years*, 191–92.

forward to the floor. One of the assassins fired three more shots at the fallen man from up close. In the audience a massive panic ensued, all the more so as the assassins also fired shots into the audience, whether in the excitement or out of fear that they could be attacked or arrested. As it later turned out, Milyukov remained uninjured. Apparently the first shots missed, and it seems Milyukov's collapse, which apparently saved his life, was caused only by the panic that broke out in the audience. Nabokov, however, died of his severe injuries immediately after the assassination. In addition, several members of the audience were wounded … After the assassination, two of the assassins got up on the stage and made excited speeches to the panicked, fleeing audience, from which it became clear that they had committed the revolver attack to take revenge on Milyukov and his party friends on the democratic left wing of the middle class for the fall of Russian monarchism. Two of the assassins were later arrested with the help of the audience, and cool-headed people just barely managed to protect them from lynch law. Then the police arrived and cleared the hall.[3]

The assassins, Tsarist officers, had traveled from Munich, where they had read in the newspaper about Milyukov's upcoming lecture. As the press reported, they showed no remorse during the police interrogation, but rather boasted about their deed.

Four successive editions of the Russian daily newspaper *Rul'* reported on the irreplaceable loss. In *Die Weltbühne* Kurt Tucholsky wrote a poem titled "Russian Competition," in which he describes the assassination and compares it to the series of murders by German monarchists.[4] In July the assassins were given prison sentences of twelve to fourteen years. That did not prevent the shooter, Sergei Taboritsky, from making a nice career later on. In the fall of 1936 Hitler named the monarchist General Biskupsky head of the Department of Émigré Affairs. Taboritsky became his undersecretary. His task was to ferret out the Russian Jews in Berlin.[5]

The murderer of his father back on the loose, this time on the hunt for the son's wife—it was this macabre twist that finally drove Véra and Vladimir out of the country in which they had remained for so long that it's hard not to think of the frog in the pot who fails to jump out of the

---

3   *Berliner Tageblatt*, no. 119, March 29, 1922 (trans. Ross Benjamin).
4   See Zimmer, *Nabokovs Berlin*, 130.
5   See *Véra*, 77, and Zimmer, *Nabokovs Berlin*, 130.

gradually heated water. And yet the atmosphere in Germany had not heated up all that slowly, and most had jumped earlier. Perhaps it was the grave in Tegel that kept Nabokov and his Jewish wife in Berlin for so long. From this grave, as the son must have perceived it, his father ultimately saved his life. In the spring of 1940 they had to flee Paris in the face of the German invasion. They had obtained visas for the United States, but they lacked the $650 they needed for the three steamer tickets. A Jewish rescue organization came to their aid, paying half the costs. The head of the organization was an old friend of Vladimir Nabokoff.[6]

The death of his father was the dark sun that irradiated all that followed in the son's life. The most moving passages in *The Gift* are about Fyodor's father, a naturalist who never returned from an expedition to Asia. One night the telephone rings unexpectedly. Fyodor leaves the house. His emotions surge at the prospect of this unhoped-for reunion— "his heart was bursting like that of a man before execution, but at the same time this execution was such a joy that life faded before it"[7]—until the author rudely awakens us and Fyodor. He had hoped all too intensely for the reunion with his father—so intensely that, since reality could not fulfill his longing, nothing could help him but a dream.

Unlike Fyodor's loss, the death of Nabokov's father had the additional sharp edge of the sudden and the violent. For the rest of his life the son never came to terms with it. Up to the end he could not speak about it. For that, there was literature. At the age of sixty, he still has the protagonist of *Pale Fire* fall victim to a misdirected assassination. His metaphysics is encapsulated in the date of this fictional incident. It would have been obvious to have the assassination occur on the day of his father's death, but Nabokov has it occur on his birthday. The switch is more than a trick or code: in this date, death and birth coincide; what seemed dead will actually live on.

---

6   See *Véra*, 104–5.
7   *The Gift*, 354.

## The Golden Egg

As he told *The New York Times* in late 1976, when he was already seriously ill, Nabokov read aloud in his "diurnal delirium" from his last, unfinished novel, *The Original of Laura*, to a small audience in his sickroom consisting of peacocks, pigeons, nurses, and his "long dead parents."[8]

It was not the first time that he turned to the dead with his fiction. Half a century earlier Nabokov had already toyed with the idea of an audience in the beyond. In 1923, a year after his father's death, he wrote the story "Gods," which gave a thinly veiled answer to the question: For whom was this author actually writing?

"Gods" is about loss, the death of a loved one. The narrator wanders through Berlin. Despite his mourning, he is in a strangely exuberant, even ecstatic mood. "How can death exist," he wonders, "when they lead camels along a springtime street?" There is no death, he repeats insistently to himself:

> The wind comes tumbling upon me from behind like a limp doll and tickles my neck with its downy paw. There can be no death.[9]

The story goes on in this style. But something about this exuberant grief, the celebration of the camels and the downy wind, is not quite suited to the supposed subject. The story has a slightly false tone. As the narration makes clear, the young man has lost his little boy. His little boy? It's hard to avoid the impression that, to distance his fiction from his life, the author inverted the generations: out of his dead father he made a dead son. But this diminishes the story's psychological credibility, because the loss of a parent is not the same as the loss of a child (or rather, the other way around). When he later had a child himself, Nabokov placed a completely different accent on the theme. The death of Adam Krug's son does not provoke lyricism about camels, but tortured madness.

The real theme—the theme of the son and his idolized father—is hidden in a little story within the story. To distract his wife from her grief,

8   *Selected Letters*, 562.
9   *Stories*, 46, 50.

the narrator tells her a historical fable: the tale of the first balloon flight over the Champs de Mars in Paris. The inventor of the first hydrogen balloon, Jacques Charles, sends his son to the market to fetch him a chicken—not for supper but to be the first balloon passenger. As the "enormous, lightweight dome" with its "gilded gondola attached by silken cords" rises into the air, the weeping father embraces his son. The next morning a peasant finds "an immense heap of motley silk" on the shore of the Loire. Nearby lies an overturned cage with a little white chicken in it. The peasant sells the silk, uses the gondola as a crib for his firstborn, and puts the chicken in the backyard. After some time has elapsed, it lays four golden eggs. The explanation is that the hen on the balloon flight "had traversed the entire flush of the sunset, and the sun, a fiery cock with a crimson crest, had done some fluttering over her."

The balloon fable and sun myth serve as a consolation to the grieving parents: "My heart, too, has soared through the dawn," the narrator tells his wife. "You and I shall have a new, golden son, a creation of your tears and my fables."[10]

As dubious as this ending may be from a literary point of view, it is exemplary in terms of the grieving process. The denial of death and the desire to transform one's tears into something else—something enduring like ore or gold—are still common techniques of dealing with grief. But Nabokov adds something uncommon. At the end of the balloon tale, the narrator turns to his wife, whose eyes have again filled with darkness in memory of their son. He urges her not to cry and declares:

> He can hear my fable, there's no doubt at all he can hear it. It is to him that it's addressed. Words have no borders. Try to understand![11]

Did he hear it? For whom did Nabokov write? He told stories for him, the departed, we may infer—and perhaps he believed that his words reached beyond the borders. The fundamental tragedy of his life was at the root of his existence as a writer. With the death of his father begins his

10   Ibid., 48–50.
11   Ibid., 49.

effervescent productivity. In two years Sirin writes twelve stories, five plays, and about eighty poems. The word *God* vanishes from his poetry. In its place begins the dance of spirits.

## A Draft from the Beyond

"This world here and now," Franz Kafka wrote in a fragment, "cannot be followed by a Beyond, for the Beyond is eternal, hence it cannot be in temporal contact with this world here and now."[12] Nabokov's fictitious philosopher Delalande expresses a similar view when he rejects the idea of a "road" that leads to the beyond and chooses instead the image of a house in which air is constantly coming in through the cracks.[13] This slight draft from the beyond wafts through Nabokov's whole oeuvre. It's only a mild exaggeration to say that his work is haunted.[14]

They don't always reveal themselves by name and encrypted messages like Cynthia and Sybil Vane; still, the ghosts are hard to miss. In *Transparent Things* it's a dead writer who welcomes the protagonist to the spirit realm after his demise. In *The Defense* a dead grandfather plays a hidden but important role. Even works that are apparently above suspicion bear the watermark that, according to Véra, was impressed on every page her husband wrote.[15] Do we know exactly where sinful Humbert is at the time of his writing? Ultimately he appeals to his jurors: "Oh, winged

---

12  Franz Kafka, *The Blue Octavo Notebooks*, 31.

13  See *The Gift*, 310. *Invitation to a Beheading* begins with an epigraph from Delalande.

14  An important early study was *Nabokov's Spectral Dimension* by W. W. Rowe. The most comprehensive is *Nabokov's Otherworld* by Vladimir E. Alexandrov. With the monograph *Nabokov's Pale Fire* Brian Boyd has provided the most recent demonstration that philological spectral photography need not lead to blurry impressions. D. Barton Johnson, who has himself contributed his fair share to this literature, has recently taken a cautiously critical stance against the metaphysical readings of Nabokov—that is, against their vogue, which seems to him to be getting out of hand. So goes the swing of the scholarly pendulum. (See D. Barton Johnson and Brian Boyd, "Prologue: The Otherworld," in *Nabokov's World*, vol. 1, 20–21.)

15  In 1979 Véra remarked in a preface to his Russian poems that the hereafter (*potustoronnost'*) "permeates all that he has written and characterizes it like a kind of watermark." (See Johnson, *Worlds in Regression*, 185.)

gentlemen of the jury!" And when he speaks of the "well-heated, albeit tombal, seclusion" in which he sets down his confession, it almost sounds like the old-fashioned Hell.[16] In *Ada* the mermaid Lucette seems to be guiding the lovers' fates from the beyond. And in *Pale Fire* Shade's daughter lives on after her suicide, as Brian Boyd seeks to prove: she flutters about her father as a butterfly.[17]

The philologists also made a find in the novel *Invitation to a Beheading*. Nabokov wrote the first draft in a two-week creative frenzy in 1934. In it, a strange little song turns up repeatedly. It sounds like it comes from an Italian opera: "*Mali é trano t'amesti*." Only the words are not Italian. Nor do they come from any other known language. And then there's the novel's protagonist, Cincinnatus, who is waiting in his cell for his beheading and almost dies of fear, but repeats insistently to himself, "I know something. I know something. But expression of it comes so hard!" What he knows is precisely what is sung in the pseudo-Italian song. It's not a line from an extraterrestrial opera, but rather an anagram of a Russian phrase. Decoded, it reads, "*smert' mila éto taina*"—"Death is sweet, [but] it's a secret."[18]

So does this secret also mean the corollary, that life is bitter? In the bleak novels *Invitation to a Beheading* and *Bend Sinister*, it certainly is. But a hidden tension between love of the world and disgust for the world marks all of Nabokov's works. His subtlest treatment of this tension is the novel *Pnin*, which he wrote to recover from the monstrous *Lolita* and which has always stood in the latter's shadow. *Pnin* is a masterpiece disguised as a minor work. Almost all the themes and motifs that we have pursued thus far are concentrated in this slender, accessible, and apparently cheerful book, which deftly conceals its abysses. In *Lolita*, as we will see, the devil is in the details. In *Pnin* it's only the squirrel. It jumps through the treetops and tries to shake us off, but we stay on its tail.

---

16   *Lolita*, 125, 308.
17   See Boyd, *Nabokov's Pale Fire,* 129–48.
18   *Invitation to a Beheading*, 103, 91. The anagram was decoded by Gennady Barabtarlo. (See *The Nabokov Research Newsletter* 9 [1982], 34–35.) Andrew Field mentions two deleted passages from a memorial article Nabokov wrote, which clearly testified to his belief in life after death (see *Life and Art*, 182–83).

# 7

## PNIN'S JOURNEY INTO THE LIGHT

In the summer of 1953 Nabokov began writing a series of stories about an unsuccessful Russian professor in America. He regarded the project as a nice, perhaps not all-too-serious trifle. It had the advantage of being printed serially in *The New Yorker*, which paid generously ($800 per installment)[1]—an opportunity that couldn't be passed up, especially since the tale of Humbert Humbert wouldn't lend itself to advance publication. Nabokov later claimed that the novel's structure had stood clearly before his eyes from the start, but his alteration of the ending indicates that the crystal ball must have been streaky here and there. What changed most in the course of the writing was his view of the protagonist. At first Timofey Pnin was no more than a colorful bird to him; the author felt no excessive sympathy for his character.[2] Accordingly, he looked forward unfeelingly to the final departure he had in mind for him. "Poor Pnin," he explained to a publisher, "dies, with everything unsettled and uncompleted, including the book Pnin had been writing all his life."[3] But in the end Pnin is hurtling out of town quite alive, and is only outwardly defeated. He is no longer "poor Pnin."[4]

---

1    See Diment, *Pniniad*, 168.
2    At this early stage Nabokov describes his protagonist as "not a very nice person but ... fun." (Boyd, *American Years*, 225.)
3    *Selected Letters*, 143.
4    In all his later comments, Nabokov stresses that Pnin "is an attractive and admirable person," and calls him "a man of great moral courage, a pure man, a scholar and a staunch friend, serenely wise, faithful to a single love." (See Ibid., 437, 182.) The somewhat blurblike character of this pitch letter to a publisher doesn't change the fact that there has been a clear shift of emphasis.

Nabokov has often been accused of all-too-openly poking fun at Mark Szeftel with the character of Pnin. In 1945 the Russian historian began teaching at Cornell. Three years later Nabokov became his colleague. Like Pnin, Szeftel was not promoted. He was the oldest assistant professor on campus and a figure of mild ridicule, not only because of his strong French-Russian accent. Nabokov could laugh himself to tears at the entertaining stories that were told about Szeftel, but at the same time he would exclaim: "What an innocent man!" Szeftel was apparently fixated on his successful Russian colleague with a mixture of envy and admiration. But his attempts to cultivate a closer connection to the Nabokovs were rebuffed. Whenever Szeftel complained that they saw each other so seldom, Vladimir would respond, "But we both know what we are working on!"[5] That was apparently enough. Aside from Véra and their son, lonely Szeftel felt bitterly, Nabokov had no need for other people. Regarding the blow *Pnin* dealt him, he remained silent even in his diary. All that is known is his wonderful, plaintive exclamation in an elevator with Nabokov: "Ve arre all Pnins!"

In 1961 Szeftel left Cornell for the University of Washington. There fortune smiled on him for once. On the faculty he found in the Russian professor Yuri Ivask, whose absentmindedness and funny English were legendary, a second potential Pnin. Ivask, too, had met Nabokov, which fueled the rumor that he was the actual model for the Waindell professor. The existence of two Pnins led to mutual exoneration. A colleague of the professors recalls having coffee once with Mr. Ivask, and Ivask told him under the pledge of secrecy that the character Pnin was actually modeled on Marc Szeftel. A week later he met Szeftel for lunch. Szeftel informed him in confidence that the prototype for Pnin was Mr. Ivask.[6]

The novel that would ultimately immortalize Szeftel is itself full of doubles and mirrorings. Though *Pnin* is far from being as sensational as *Lolita*, it is scarcely less complex. The readings it invites are as abundant as the multiple interpretations of *Sebastian Knight*. *Pnin* can be read as an

---

5 Diment, *Pniniad*, 36.
6 All Szeftel details are from Galya Diment's superb study *Pniniad*. For Szeftel's exclamation in the elevator, see also Field, *Life and Art*, 291.

autobiographically tinged exile novel or a campus novel—it is undoubtedly the greatest of that genre, even if the term did not yet exist at the
time. *Pnin* is a hidden modern doctrine of the elements,[7] a satire of
Freudian pedagogy (the weakest aspect of the book), a homage to
Aleksandr Pushkin[8]—and perhaps it is the very work that its protagonist is
writing, the *Petite Histoire* of Russian culture in which the *Grande Histoire*
would be reflected in miniature.

Indeed, the whole book is a mirror construction. It is divided into
seven chapters with the axis of symmetry running through the fourth: that
is, the first chapter is reflected in the seventh, the second in the sixth, and
the third in the fifth. The first chapter ends with Pnin's lecture in
Cremona, as does the last. In the second chapter Pnin moves into a new
room; in the sixth he moves into his new house. In the third chapter we
witness a day of his work—on Pnin's birthday, though no one realizes;[9] in

---

7  Consider the balanced distribution of fire, air, water, and earth. Eric Wind is the
name of the second husband of Pnin's wife, Liza. As the "land father," Wind is also
identified with the element of earth. It is not only as the "water father" that Pnin is
linked to water (from which his wife rises as a mermaid): there's also the squirrel that
desires water from the drinking fountain, and it is on the water that Pnin learns of Liza's
betrayal. A vibrating fan almost falls into his bathtub. Victor's gift, the glass bowl,
almost shatters in his sink. Pnin's less successful gift for Victor, a soccer ball, ends up in a
rain-swollen brook. Victor's second water father, his art teacher, bears the name Lake.
The Great Moscow Fire, which Pnin recalls after his first seizure, provides the element
of fire, but so too does his idiosyncratic pronunciation, which makes Mrs. Thayer into
Mrs. Fire.
8  Pushkin is not merely a subject of Pnin's lectures and flights of thought. He is
omnipresent in the novel. There's a mysterious connection between the anniversary of
Pushkin's death and Pnin's birthday. *Eugene Onegin* is also the novel's key formal
model: "Up to this stanza Pushkin had been haunting the canto but not actually
appearing in it as a person in a novel. Pushkin's voice had been heard and his presence
felt, as he flitted in and out of the stanzas in a ghostly atmosphere of recollection and
nostalgia, but Onegin was not aware of his fellow rake at the ballet or in the ballroom.
Henceforth Pushkin will be a full-fledged character, and he and Onegin will actually
appear as two persons for the space of four stanzas ..." (*Eugene Onegin: A Novel in Verse*,
25.) If we replace "Pushkin" with "N." and "Onegin" with "Pnin," we get the formal
principle of the involved narrator who appears onstage in flesh and blood at the end but
beforehand follows his character into the ballroom and in N.'s case even into the
bathroom.
9  Nabokov gives us dates and clues so that we can celebrate this birthday at least

the fifth chapter a day of his vacation. And in the fourth chapter? Whatever might be hidden at this core, through which the invisible central axis runs, must have been important to the architect.

## The Ashes of History

*Pnin* is also a realistic novel of its time. No other work by Nabokov lets so much contemporary history pass through its membranes. This history seeps in virtually unnoticed. Unlike in *Bend Sinister* or *Invitation to a Beheading*, Nabokov does not enlist it in the service of political allegory. For that very reason *Pnin* is—alongside *Lolita*—his historically richest book. The fifties of Eisenhower and McCarthy are completely preserved in it, as is the first half of the century: old Russia, Lenin and Trotsky, Hitler's Germany and exile, the arrival of immigrants on Ellis Island and the mushroom cloud over Hiroshima, of which Pnin is reminded by the thought bubble of a comic. And the historical echo chamber extends still further into the past. Pnin plans his final seminar on the subject of tyranny in general, Nicholas the First, the massacre of the Armenians, the colonists in Africa. But Pnin's conclusion is anthropological—not to say

---

belatedly. In the first chapter the narrator works in the fact that Pnin's birthday is on February 15 (according to the Gregorian calendar). In the third chapter we are first reminded that Pnin no longer celebrates his birthday according to the Julian calendar. Then we follow him into the library, where he glances at the latest issue of a Russian-language émigré newspaper—"Saturday, February 12—and this was Tuesday, O Careless Reader!" (*Pnin*, 75.) Therefore, it is February 15, Pnin's birthday—and not even he celebrates it! Dieter E. Zimmer points out in his commentary to *Pnin* (Rowohlt) that February 15 of the year in question did not fall on a Tuesday, unlike the anniversary of Pushkin's death, which is accorded similar thematic importance and actually falls on the Tuesday of February 10. Complicated! The solution to the riddle leads us back to the Cornell campus. As Diment demonstrates, the variances between the earlier *New Yorker* version and the book version of *Pnin* tend in a clear direction: Pnin's basic biographical information is aligned with Szeftel's. And Pnin's birthday is suspiciously close to that of his prototype. Szeftel's birthday was on February 10, and February 10 in fact fell that year on a Tuesday, which permits the conclusion that Nabokov momentarily confused fiction and reality and looked up the date of Szeftel's actual birthday on the calendar. His notes in which he determined the dates for *Pnin* seem to confirm this reassuringly human explanation. (See *Pniniad*, 46, 169–70.)

Schopenhauerian—rather than narrowly historical: "The history of man," he explains to his department head, Professor Hagen, "is the history of pain."[10]

We no longer have any illusions about the caustic irony of the fact that it is the German professor Hagen to whom Pnin makes this remark. It's no accident that Pnin's interlocutor bears the name of the treacherous, murderous villain from the *Nibelungenlied*. Figuratively speaking, he gives Pnin the deathblow when he informs him—at the end of the most enchanting "house-heating" party in all of literature[11]—that he is being fired. And on the whole he is more dubious than he appears at first glance. In the description of Pnin's big housewarming party, Nabokov mentions a bunch of grapes four times—why? So that Hagen can stub out his messy cigar in it at the end of the party. Basically, that says it all about him. But what renders the final judgment on him is something else. When the conversation turns to the Buchenwald concentration camp, Hagen laments above all that it had to be built so close to Weimar.[12]

Nabokov had originally intended to write in *Pnin* about the concentration camps.[13] He did not abandon this theme, but only veiled it slightly. For half a page in the fifth chapter, Pnin imagines the death of Mira, the love of his youth, in Buchenwald. Mira dies many possible deaths and is resurrected again and again to die a new one, "led away by a trained nurse, inoculated with filth, tetanus bacilli,[14] broken glass, gassed in a sham shower bath with prussic acid, burned alive in a pit on a gasoline-soaked pile of beechwood."[15] This half a page is the black heart and actual moral center of the book. Neither Pnin nor Nabokov, who had to envision

---

10   *Pnin*, 168.

11   Ibid., 151. This particular host's version of a "housewarming party."

12   See ibid., 135.

13   Field, *Life and Art*, 104. Kuzmanovich relates Sergei's death to the torture and death that Nabokov has Adam Krug's son, David, suffer in *Bend Sinister*, contrary to his earlier plans. (See Kuzmanovich, "Suffer the Little Children," in *Nabokov at Cornell*, 49–57.)

14   In Neuengamme the Nazis conducted experiments on the prisoners with tuberculosis pathogens. See Grossman, "The Gay Nabokov."

15   *Pnin*, 135.

Sergei's end in Neuengamme, gets over these deaths. Mira's ashes are omnipresent—in Pushkin's mournful verses on the "refrigerated ashes,"[16] and even in the speck of coal dust that enters the narrator's eye and has to be removed by Pnin's father.

We have already noted the diabolical, fairy-tale qualities of the speck of coal dust—it was the punishment for hubris and infected its victim with hubris. But who is this narrator named Vladimir anyway? He is an almost omniscient first-person narrator, like the narrator in Proust. What is odd is the "almost." The first-person narrator of *In Search of Lost Time* often knows the most intimate thoughts of his characters, but at other times he has to entangle himself in webs of hypotheses, as if the glimpse into other souls were suddenly barred to him. Vladimir N. in *Pnin* is quite similar. On the one hand, he even knows what Pnin dreams, and thus perhaps more than Pnin himself, who might have forgotten his dream by the next morning. On the other hand, his omniscience is sometimes suspended, at which point he has to guess and make suppositions, as he does regarding the true reason for Pnin's repeated heart attacks. This Olympian narrator and creator of a world is a fallible, dubious God, who shouldn't be surprised if his creatures rebel against him—without much chance of success, for in the end it's still Vladimir who tells their story.

That he is not a disembodied authorial spirit but rather must be a particular person is evident even before he says "I" for the first time. He has to be a Russian, for he doesn't speak of miles, but rather of versts.[17] Shortly thereafter he calls Pnin his friend. In the second chapter he almost slips and reveals himself to be the litterateur with whom Pnin's later wife, Liza, had a "rather silly affair."[18] In the sixth chapter he lets himself be introduced as a "prominent Anglo-Russian writer" and "really fascinating lecturer." None other than he himself later praises the "unusual lucidity and strength" of his memory.[19]

---

16  Ibid., 68.

17  Ibid., 8.

18  Ibid., 45.

19  Ibid., 140, 169, 179–80.

This Vladimir N.—who does not appear onstage in person until the seventh chapter—obviously has a slight tendency to boast. His model airplane is not only twice as big as Timofey's, but he also bought it in Biarritz.[20] What a snob! Despite the similarity of names, Nabokov has as much or as little to do with this narrator as he does with Pnin.[21] He transferred his own strengths and weaknesses onto both characters. And yet, neither is any less fictitious.

In any case, the day Vladimir entered his life was not a good day for Pnin. The narrator always comes out ahead of him: first he has an affair with Liza, which Pnin will never forgive him; then he gets the prominent post we all would have wished for Pnin. Should we trust this man—and do we have a choice? For Vladimir, even if he shares many outward traits with Nabokov, is not necessarily trustworthy. He pats his supposed friend on the back somewhat too condescendingly, his memory doesn't always seem so exceptional,[22] and he elegantly skirts his role in the affair with Liza—still, he is to blame for her suicide attempt.

The empirical Vladimir Nabokov appears only twice in this book. Once it's in a discussion of the exile author "Sirin," under the pseudonym of his early years.[23] The second time he's hiding in the description of the little blue butterfly that Pnin and his Russian colleague Chateau find by the river on their vacation. It is a *Lycaeides melissa samuelis Nabokov*.[24]

---

20  Ibid., 177. See also Kelly, "Nabokov, Snobizm and Selfhood in *Pnin*," in *Nabokov's World*, vol. 1, 117–40.

21  Szeftel was not the only model for Pnin. On the Cornell campus Nabokov himself was "considered a kind of Pnin-figure." The outward similiarities are considerable. Both arrive in the United States in 1940 and become citizens in 1945. Pnin is a year older than Nabokov. Both love Pushkin and Lermontov. Both endure protracted dental operations and ultimately wear dentures. Both are sensitive to noise and drive badly or not at all. Pnin's comments on *Anna Karenina* and his interest in gestures are those of his creator. Both have a shadow behind the heart. (See Diment, *Pniniad*, 9, 48–49.)

22  At least Pnin claims that N. invents all sorts of things, such as the good marks in algebra that Pnin never actually received. (*Pnin*, 180, 185.)

23  Ibid., 117.

24  Ibid., 128. See Zimmer, *A Guide to Nabokov's Butterflies and Moths*, 166.

## Glass Shoes Made of Fur

The speck in the narrator's eye is not the only particle in the novel from the land of fairy tales. Pnin's ex-wife, Liza, is described as a mermaid, but the designation applies much better to Pnin himself. Does he not live as chastely as the mermaid under water? The mermaid has human legs and genitalia only on land. It is thus with good reason that Pnin is given the strange label "water father," while Eric Wind, the biological father of Liza's son, calls himself "land father."[25]

But we have not yet left the circle of fairy tales. On the first page the narrator mentions Pnin's almost feminine feet. These little feet belong to a character from a friendlier fairy tale, which comes to the fore in the second half of the novel. It is the tale of Cinderella. In contrast to the little mermaid, Cinderella lives happily ever after with her prince. During the day she stands in the shadow of her scornful sisters; in the evening she is the most beautiful woman at the ball and wins the prince's heart. One would be inclined to say that only the first part of the fairy tale applies to Pnin. He is the Cinderella of Waindell, and only the Clementses appreciate his true qualities. But he has the small feet that are decisive in the end. Pnin makes the famous story of Cinderella's glass shoe into the topic of a little private lecture at his party: quite the conversationalist, he enlightens his guests about the misunderstanding on which the story of the glass shoe is based. Originally the shoe that fits Cinderella is not made of *verre*, or glass, but rather of *vair*, or fur. To be precise: squirrel fur.[26]

---

25 *Pnin*, 55. Priscilla Meyer's essay on Nabokov's spirits illuminates the metaphysical background of the strange dual designation by tracing it to its literary source: *The Water Babies* (1862) by Charles Kingsley. The poet, spiritualist, and chaplain to Queen Victoria, who is smuggled into *Pale Fire*, seems to have more in common with the mad commentator Charles Kinbote than just the first ten letters of his name. (See Meyer, "Nabokov and the Spirits," 92–93.)

26 *Pnin*, 158. Lucette, too, the mermaid of *Ada*, thinks of her "vair-furred bedroom slippers" shortly before she drowns. This shows how closely one fairy-tale character is linked to another. The mermaid Lucette wears glass shoes. For the allusions to Cinderella running through the whole novel, see *Ada*, 12, 49, 114, 228, 248, 334, 373, 374, 401, 494.

With this aside Pnin ties up a number of thematic loose ends. His etymological digression links Cinderella to the departed Mira: Cinderella's shoe is made of squirrel fur, and Mira's surname, Belochkin, contains the Russian word for squirrel, *belochka*.

Undoubtedly, Mira's horrible death seems not at all suited to a fairy tale in which everything turns out wonderfully in the end. And yet Nabokov does everything he can to reinforce this connection. What makes Pnin think of the topic of Cinderella in the first place is a remark about his glass bowl, which was a gift from Liza's son, Victor. The color of the bowl reminds one of his party guests of Cinderella's glass shoes. Thus the Cinderella motif encompasses Pnin's old love for Mira and his new, paternal love for Victor. In both cases something in this love resists annihilation. No one who has read the novel will forget the moment when Pnin has a mishap while doing the dishes after the party. An object falls into the sink, a splinter of glass stings him—but Victor's bowl is intact. Nabokov manages to make us sigh with as much relief as if the Holy Grail had been at stake.

That doesn't mean we would go so far as to lend the survival of this bowl metaphysical significance. Perhaps *we* wouldn't, but Nabokov does exactly that. In the middle of the axis chapter—and indeed in the exact middle, on page 96 of 191 pages—he reveals the secret of the color spectrum. In fact, he explains, this spectrum is not a circle, but a spiral of tints. The last of these colors are "Cinderella shades transcending human perception."[27] Transcendence—that's precisely what all the allusions to fairy tales are about.

And they're about love in its heroic form. Timofey remains faithful to Liza, who treats him worse than anyone else does.[28] His love for her is free

---

27  *Pnin*, 96.

28  Consider what Liza permits herself in the second chapter alone. She announces her visit to Waindell without stating the reason. Pnin is flooded with happiness when he picks her up at the bus station. She ridicules his clothing and his apartment and conducts a whole conversation with him that inevitably gives him false hopes. He rolls with laughter when Liza calls him "water father"—an exuberant reaction to her statement just beforehand that she no longer loves Eric Wind. What is he supposed to think other than that she wants to come back to him? "His eyes were like stars and quite

of egoism and free of the desire that figures so darkly in *Lolita* and *Ada*. But since this love is as hopeless as that of the mermaid, it would destroy Pnin if a second love did not supplement it, as pure as the first and as free of egoism, even the natural egoism of the father—for the son Pnin loves is not his biological son. This second love, which unfolds in the central chapter, gives Pnin new heart. Consequently, the atmosphere changes after this fourth chapter, the mermaid withdraws, and the focus shifts onto Cinderella's shoe. To the right of the axis of reflection things have brightened up.[29] The glass bowl only *almost* shatters, and after learning that he's being fired Pnin writes his letter to Hagen with a "firm hand."[30]

It is not only in his selfless love that Timofey—who incidentally is completely humorless—stirs a few religious memories. What are the traditional characteristics of a saint? He is chaste; he is good to animals; the simple folk admire him. Often he suffers martyrdom, is transfigured, and enters God's light. Pnin is explicitly called a saint by two characters: by Liza, even if it is for the wrong reasons, and by Desdemona, the Clementses' charwoman, who gossips daily with God, so she should know. At the very beginning, the narrator's gaze falls upon Pnin's chaste hand.[31] No other Nabokovian protagonist is as chaste as Pnin—the classic countercharacter (with a surprising number of points of contact) to the satyr Humbert Humbert.[32] Even in his deepest sorrow Pnin thinks of the

---

wet." Her next question, too, about how much he earns, the poor man cannot help interpreting along these lines, and Liza torments him for a while longer by reciting her bad poetry before she discloses the real reason for her visit: she wants Pnin to support young Victor. Liza's profound cruelty in this scene again provokes the question whether there's not a streak of misogyny running through Nabokov's work.

29 See Connolly, "Pnin: The Wonder of Recurrence and Transformation," in *Nabokov's Fifth Arc*, 195–210. Connolly shows how the dynamic changes after the fourth chapter and how some of Victor's genius overflows onto Pnin, enabling him to escape the compulsive patterns, which take on a friendly significance. To offer just one example: in the third chapter Pnin thinks gloomily of Pushkin's verse on death, which could befall him in the waves as well; in the fifth he swims in the river, puffing and dignified.

30 *Pnin,* 173.

31 Ibid., 184, 40, 8.

32 It's remarkable how much Pnin has in common not only with Marc Szeftel and V.N., but also with Humbert Humbert. Pnin's relationship with Victor mirrors

needs of other creatures—he gives a pushy squirrel water, and he scrapes together leftovers for the little white dog in his new neighborhood, even though he has just found out he's being fired: "There was no reason a human's misfortune should interfere with a canine's pleasure." The same little dog looks out the window of the pale blue sedan in which Pnin leaves Waindell in the novel's concluding image.[33]

Pnin has enemies and deriders, and like all saints he has devotees among the simple folk. The man who rents him a room, Clements, is a true friend who seems to have climbed out of a Van Eyck painting. He resembles Canon van der Paele, who in Van Eyck's famous painting kneels before the Madonna and Christ child.[34] Surely it would have been just as easy for Nabokov to find a secular painting to use as a model. But he scatters still other little sacred lights throughout the novel. Pnin experiences his major dental operation as death and rebirth. There is a reference in the scene to his "martyred mouth."[35] With his new set of teeth Pnin feels like a "reformed man." That he appears "transfigured" during a croquet game also belongs to the layer of religious language that Nabokov surreptitiously slips into the novel.[36]

The thematic strand of creation, procreation, and birth runs through the book from the first chapter. It is almost imperceptibly linked to Pnin's strange heart attacks. Pnin's wave of faintness in the first chapter is brought

---

Humbert's with Lolita. Both children are the same age when they enter the lives of their stepfathers. Both are on their own: Lolita's mother is dead, Victor's absent. As a surrogate father, Pnin succeeds precisely where Humbert fails. Victor has all the qualities that Humbert finds lacking in Lolita. Both have a fairy-tale model symbolized in a gift exchanged between father and stepchild: Andersen's mermaid in Lolita's case; the bowl in the Cinderella color in Victor's case. Both stepfathers cannot forget a deceased love from their early youth. Both get married in Paris, and both marriages fail. Both are betrayed by their first wives. Both hear the dreaded words for a husband's ears shortly before or during the journey by ship to America. Both immigrate to the United States, write scholarly works, and suffer from heart problems. Both are melancholics who have fallen hopelessly in love.

33  Ibid., 171, 190–91.
34  Ibid., 154.
35  Ibid., 38.
36  Ibid., 39, 130.

on by the circumstance that he doesn't have his valise with his lecture notes and therefore has to get off the bus in all haste. But the only reason he doesn't have his valise is that the train station employee with whom he deposited it had to drive his wife to the maternity hospital—prematurely, as we learn: his wife's delivery was delayed.

So at the beginning of the novel there's already a problematic birth. Nor is Victor's birth completely cut-and-dried, for he has two fathers: a spiritual water father, who did not participate in the act of procreation, and his material, true, extremely dubious land father, Dr. Wind. Nabokov thereby introduces the motif of a staggered procreation, so to speak. But wait! There, jumping through the treetops—isn't that the animal that keeps bothering Timofey?

## The Shadow of the Squirrel

Every reader of this novel notices that a squirrel shows up in it more often than chance would permit—to be precise, an American gray squirrel, *Sciurus carolinensis*. Since every American campus is teeming with gray squirrels, they are part of the local color. Still, their appearances are too precisely choreographed for readers not to wonder what's hidden behind them. There is no chapter in which the gray squirrel doesn't make a brief appearance. And each time it comes as the witness or perhaps herald—if not the trigger—of significant and often ambiguous events in the life of the protagonist.

In the first chapter, on his obstacle-laden trip to Cremona, Pnin ends up in a park in the small town of Whitchurch. The place is already subtly sacralized by the church in its name, and the park reminds Pnin of a cemetery.[37] In this park Pnin suffers the first of his mysterious, mystical seizures—a fall through a trapdoor in the present that transports him deep into his childhood. He barely manages to sit down on a stone bench before he slides into the past and sees himself as an eleven-year-old delirious with fever. Beside his bed is a folding screen, and he stares at the

---

37  Ibid., 19.

picture on it of an "old man hunched up on a bench, and a squirrel holding a reddish object in its front paws":

> Timosha, a methodical child, had often wondered what that object could be (a nut? a pine cone?), and now that he had nothing else to do, he set himself to solve this dreary riddle, but the fever that hummed in his head drowned every effort in pain and panic.

When, after further fruitless attempts to decipher his wallpaper pattern, Pnin awakes from his trance, he is no longer alone: "A gray squirrel sitting on comfortable haunches on the ground before him was sampling a peach stone."[38]

Quite inconspicuous, this first appearance, and yet not without significance. Let us try to be as methodical as young Timofey and identify what is presented in this scene. The gray squirrel is there when the veil of time is lifted and past and present merge. It is there as more than just a chance observer of the scene: like an emblem, it displays the solution to the riddle that Pnin seeks in his fever dream. He himself is the old man hunched up on the park bench, and the red object is obviously the very peach stone that the squirrel is holding in its paws.[39]

In the second chapter, too, the squirrel appears to Pnin in a park. Pnin is in a desolate state: after Liza's visit, his hope that she would come back to him has been dashed once and for all. Now he has nothing left in the world, as he declares at the end of the chapter. On his way through the park he muses that even in a hereafter in which he doesn't believe he would be defenselessly subjected to Liza's soul. Then the following occurs:

> He seemed to be quite unexpectedly (for human despair seldom leads to great truths) on the verge of a simple solution of the universe but was interrupted by an urgent request. A squirrel under a tree had seen Pnin on the path. In one sinuous tendril-like movement, the intelligent animal climbed up to the brim of a drinking fountain and, as Pnin approached,

---

38   Ibid., 23, 25.
39   See also Meyer, "Nabokov and the Spirits," 90–91.

thrust its oval face toward him with a rather coarse spluttering sound, its cheeks puffed out. Pnin understood and after some fumbling he found what had to be pressed for the necessary results. Eyeing him with contempt, the thirsty rodent forthwith began to sample the stocky sparkling pillar of water, and went on drinking for a considerable time. "She has a fever, perhaps," thought Pnin, weeping quietly and freely, and all the time politely pressing the contraption down while trying not to meet the unpleasant eye fixed upon him. Its thirst quenched, the squirrel departed without the least sign of gratitude.[40]

That Pnin makes the gender-neutral animal into a "she" is explained by his mental preoccupation with Liza, who has just treated him exactly as the squirrel does—she too wanted something from him, demanded it quite condescendingly, and no sooner had he fulfilled her wish than she left him without the least sign of gratitude. The similarity between the consecutive plot points seems to suggest a connection between Liza and the feminine squirrel. But the reader may think of another woman here too. Why would the squirrel have a fever? The last person to have a fever was Pnin as a child. Because of this high fever the family called in a pediatrician, who examined Timofey. And this doctor was none other than the father of Mira Belochkin, of whose many deaths Pnin must not think if he wants to go on living.

In the third chapter, on the icy path to the college library, Pnin sees a flock of pigeons and a squirrel—and sure enough, he slips. Two things about this scene are noteworthy. First, this time the squirrel seems to anticipate the near future as a sort of harbinger: "The squirrel, invisible now in a crotch, chattered, scolding the delinquents who would pot him out of his tree."[41] At the end of the chapter Pnin, like the squirrel, will be cast out of his dwelling: the Clementses' daughter returns to her parental home after a failed marriage, and Pnin has to look for a new abode.

And the wintry harbinger of misfortune presages something else as well. Pnin sees the squirrel dash across the multihued shadow of a tree. The colors of shadows, we find out in the next chapter, are a

---

40   *Pnin*, 58.
41   Ibid., 73.

phenomenon that Victor could distinguish when he was still a child. In the same chapter we learn that the first postcard that Pnin sends to Victor has a picture of the gray squirrel. As in the case of Cinderella's shoe, Pnin's etymological explanation provides a thematic crystallization. The word *squirrel* comes from the Greek and means "shadow-tail."[42] This not only recalls the shadow behind Pnin's heart, which his doctors discover on his X-rays and which is supposed to explain his strange seizures[43]; since the Greeks, shadows—or shades—signify ghosts.

In the fifth chapter the shade comes back to life. Pnin recalls his last encounter with Mira, in the early thirties in a Berlin restaurant. By then Mira was married, but was still exactly as Pnin remembered her: "the contour of her prominent cheekbones, and the elongated eyes, and the slenderness of arm and ankle were unchanged, were immortal."[44] We can leave aside whether the shape of her eyes and her ankles don't themselves suggest something squirrel-like. We have to take seriously, however, the fact that they are not only unchanged, but also immortal. Whether Mira's marriage would have been happy even under other historical circumstances we may, incidentally, have reason to doubt, for her husband is a fur dealer. The woman with the squirrel in her name could never feel completely safe by his side. We learn how squirrel fur relates to Cinderella's glass shoe and Pnin's love for Victor in the next, sixth, chapter. In the seventh and last chapter, the squirrel ultimately appears in Pnin's childhood room—stuffed and thereby harmless.

But isn't all this somewhat confusing? The deeper we penetrate into the novel and its thicket of motifs, the more disoriented we become. Let us clear two possible paths. Scholars have argued that Mira Belochkin, reincarnated in the squirrel, watches over Pnin's life and steers him in a favorable direction at difficult moments.[45] This view has several points in its favor. It wouldn't be the first time in Nabokov's fiction that a dead loved one appeared in the form of a small animal—and after all, it doesn't

---

42   Ibid., 88.
43   Ibid., 126.
44   Ibid.,134.
45   See Rowe, *Nabokov's Spectral Dimension*, 62ff.

always have to be a butterfly. From her treetops Mira would now and then give the lonely protagonist a helpful sign. To some extent, however, this reading whitewashes the gray squirrel: like the *Vanessa atalanta* in *Pale Fire* it would be a friendly messenger from the realm of the dead.

There are a few indications that this interpretation is too charitable. Ironically, the squirrel reveals its true nature in the only scene in which it remains invisible.

## Too Lucid

Pnin is on his way to the vacation retreat known as "The Pines," but he's lost in a maze of forest roads. He's not the only one with problems—an ant has its own troubles. After a long climb up a lookout tower, it has reached the balustrade at the top and now no longer quite knows how to proceed:

> Presently, however, a gun shot popped, and a twig leaped into the sky. The dense upper boughs in that part of the otherwise stirless forest started to move in a receding sequence of shakes or jumps, with a swinging lilt from tree to tree, after which all was still again. Another minute passed, and then everything happened at once: the ant found an upright beam leading to the roof of the tower and started to ascend it with renewed zest; the sun appeared; and Pnin at the height of hopelessness, found himself on a paved road with a rusty but still glistening sign directing wayfarers "To The Pines."[46]

Nabokov, who leaves no thread untied, mentions a few pages later as the third hobby of the Pines factotum (after bookbinding and the making of fruit liqueurs) the killing of small forest animals.[47] Thus he reveals the source of the shot. With all due sympathy for small forest animals, the passage gives us clear information. What exactly happened? First everything is going wrong; then suddenly everything is going smoothly. Not because the squirrel appears, as one might think at first reading—but

---

46   *Pnin*, 115.
47   Ibid., 119.

rather because it is driven away by the shot of the Russian recreational hunter. A minute elapses, and only then does the sun come out, and Pnin and the ant find their way.

The light comes out when the invisible, ruling demon is driven away—that provides a clue to another, darker reading of the whole novel. Perhaps the best approach to this last layer of meaning is to return to the beginning once again, to young Timofey's fever dream. After his failed attempt to solve the riddle of the squirrel on the folding screen, Pnin becomes hopelessly absorbed in his wallpaper. The pattern of the wallpaper has a particular system, but the feverish child is unable to decipher the hidden order:

> [I]f the evil designer—the destroyer of minds, the friend of fever—had concealed the key of the pattern with such monstrous care, that key must be as precious as life itself and, when found, would regain for Timofey Pnin his everyday health, his everyday world; and this lucid—alas, too lucid—thought forced him to persevere in the struggle.[48]

Like lucid Pnin, whoever searches for the key and the solution is engaged in a hard struggle against a world ruled by an evil designer. There is light in the word *lucid*. And "evil designer"—that's the key term of a Gnostic worldview.

The classic defining feature of this Gnostic view is the answer to the question of evil in Creation. How can there be such monstrousness in the world if a good God created it? The Gnostic answer is that there is not one Creator, but two—in Pninian terms one could say a water father and a land father. The true God is concealed in his realm of light. The affairs of the material world are handled by the secondary Creator God, the Demiurge. This Demiurge can by no means be trusted. In his neo-Platonic form, he is just what young Timofey fears: an evil designer. The Demiurge is powerful and bars humanity's way to its true purpose. He made the wallpaper with the patterns that only confuse us. In Gnostic imagery he is the jailer who holds us captive in the prison of matter.

---

48    Ibid., 23–24.

Whoever wants to outsmart the Demiurge must break out of this jail. Only the escape from the prison of the body leads the soul into the other-worldly realm of light. At most, sparks of this light are scattered in the material world.[49]

Does this mean that all Gnostics should commit suicide? It's not as bad as all that: they can guard the divine sparks and devote themselves to mystical illumination. For it is only through divine intuition, not through any revealed scripture, that humanity gains an intimation of its secret and its mission. The nature of the secret doctrine—immortalized in Goethe's line from "Blessed Longing": "Tell no one, only the wise"—is as characteristic of Gnostic currents as the rejection of all organized religion.

If one defines these currents issuing from antiquity widely enough, they ultimately encompass Schopenhauer's doctrine as well. His suspicion of the evil world of the will, which is concentrated in the focal point of the genitals[50] and from which one is only released in a light of which the sunlight is but a shadow—this general suspicion is nothing if not Gnostic. Thus Thomas Mann is a good disciple of Schopenhauer when he begins his *Joseph* with the Gnostic prelude "Descent into Hell."

But it was not through the despised German author that Nabokov was acquainted with mystical, Gnostic currents. Rather it was through his beloved Russian authors, such as Aleksandr Blok or Andrei Bely, whose *Petersburg* he counted among the three greatest novels of the twentieth century. In Nabokov's work the Gnostic undercurrent can be found at its strongest in the novel *Invitation to a Beheading* and the 1947 story "Signs and Symbols," which already anticipates many of *Pnin*'s themes in a nutshell.

---

49  It goes without saying that this is only a highly simplified version of what is in actuality an extremely complex form of thought and faith. In an evaluation of the respective positions of Barabtarlo, D. Barton Johnson, and Alexandrov, Timothy Langen reflects on the advantages and disadvantages of characterizing Nabokov as either Gnostic or neo-Platonic. (See "The Ins and Outs of *Invitation to a Beheading*" in *Nabokov Studies* 8, 64.)

50  See *The World as Will and Representation*, vol. I, 330 ("the genitals are the real *focus* of the will"; italics in original).

## The Evil Creator: Signs and Symbols

For this story, the greatest and saddest in his oeuvre, Nabokov had prepared for a long time. The 1924 tale "A Matter of Chance" can be regarded as the earliest preliminary study for it. That story's plot is constructed like a chess trap that ensures that, at the end, on the verge of a happy resolution, fate takes the worst possible turn. The young Mrs. Luzhin, who has lost track of her husband in the confusion of the Revolution, ends up in a compartment of the night train on which Luzhin is now working as a waiter. There's every indication that this coincidence will reunite them, but then the demonic countercoincidences accumulate. She loses her wedding ring, which lands right under Luzhin's nose, but before he can notice it, his German colleague pockets it; she makes her way to the dining car, where he would serve her, but just as she is about to enter she turns around because she's harassed by another passenger. Everything conspires fiendishly so that this couple divided by a few yards will not reunite and the husband will ultimately throw himself under the train.

The world that permits such chains of coincidences is not the best of all possible worlds, but rather the most perfidious. Against an extremely dark historical backdrop, this is also the message of the story "Signs and Symbols." An old Jewish married couple from Russia, leading a miserable immigrant life in the United States, buys a basket with ten different fruit jellies for their adult son, who has been in a sanatorium for the mentally ill for years. But they are unable to give him the gift, because he has once again tried to kill himself. In pouring rain the parents return home. The mother thinks of the endless sufferings that she and her husband must bear. The old man can't sleep, and sitting together late at night, they conceive a plan to take the young man out of the clinic and bring him home, where he'll be safer. If they take turns attending to him and lock the knives in drawers, things will somehow work out. Twice they're startled when the telephone rings. It's an unknown girl who has dialed the wrong number. The second time the woman explains to her that she's dialing the letter O instead of the zero.

Relieved by their new decision, they prepare a festive midnight tea. The birthday present stands on the table. The old man examines it with pleasure, puts on his glasses, and reads the labels of the jellies:

> His clumsy moist lips spelled out their eloquent labels: apricot, grape, beech plum, quince. He had got to crab apple, when the telephone rang again.[51]

That is the final sentence. And this time, we know, it is the call from the clinic, which will notify them of the death of their all-too-lucid son, who just managed to escape the world before his parents could bring him home. From the start, everything in the story—which reflects the theme of referential mania so artfully that everything conspires in it as well—converges on this horrible blank space.[52]

---

51  *Stories*, 603.

52  This reading is regarded as unsubtle, but unlike most scholars, I find it compelling. According to the subtle interpretation, we as readers have already fallen for Nabokov's metafictional game if we, like the insane son, piece together the signs and symbols into an unambiguous message and combinationally close the gap with which the story ends. But the narrative's elemental rhythmic effect testifies against this metafictional pluralism, which seems strangely pallid in the face of this antitheodicy disguised as a story. As in the story of Job—or Flaubert's "Un Coeur simple," which might have provided the rhythm for Nabokov's tale—in "Signs and Symbols" one loss inexorably follows another: "for after all living did mean accepting the loss of one joy after another, not even joys in her case—mere possibilities of improvement." (Ibid., 601.) That is the logic of the story, which breaks off before the last hope is annihilated. In addition to the ominous foreshadowings, Nabokov leaves ample realistic clues that the plot ends with the suicide. From the beginning the tale suggests that the son will repeat the suicide attempt. We learn that he comes up with new methods all the time and is prevented by his fellow patients from carrying them out only by chance. We learn that the sanatorium is understaffed. Thus there is an objective danger that the son, only poorly supervised in his room, will seize the opportunity once again. Moreover, we know that the third late-night phone call can no longer be from the girl dialing the wrong number: the frightened mother has explained to her about her mix-up of the zero and the O. Nabokov did not have to include this tiny plot point if he had wanted to leave the ending open. But who else would be calling the lonely couple after midnight? There is another hint that the ending is only apparently left open: the compositional doubling of a related work. "On the night of March 28, 1922, around ten o'clock, in the living room where as usual my mother was reclining on the red-plush corner couch, I happened to be reading to her Blok's verse on Italy—had just got

Read from the vantage of the ending, everything in the tale is ominous. As in the son's mania, in which even trees and clouds whisper about him, all the details on these five pages combine into a portent: the plot takes place on a rainy Friday; the underground train gets stuck; in the bus a girl is weeping on the shoulder of an older woman; a half-dead bird is twitching in a puddle; a key is forgotten; the nine and ace of spades fall from a deck of cards; a photo of a German maid with her fat fiancé slips out of an album; in the window across the street there's a man dressed in black—a chain of signs and symbols at the end of which a telephone rends the silence for the third time.

It is not the world redeemed by Christ that Nabokov depicts. It is the world of an evil designer, a world that one can escape only by tearing a hole in it.[53] Like Pnin, the paranoid son is tormented by patterns that conceal secret messages; like Pnin, as a child he is afraid of the wallpaper and avoids eye contact with a squirrel; and like the feverish Pnin, he witnesses harmless objects turn into "hives of evil."[54] Like Pnin, the sick son has only narrowly escaped the historical hive of evil. What comprises half a page in the novel is only one sentence in "Signs and Symbols." It comes when the mother is flipping through her old photo album in the evening:

---

to the end of the little poem about Florence, which Blok compares to the delicate, smoky bloom of an iris, and she was saying over her knitting, 'Yes, yes, Florence does look like a *dimnïy iris*, how true! I remember—' when the telephone rang." That is how Nabokov describes in his autobiography receiving the news of his father's murder. Or rather: that is how he omits the description. The passage ends abruptly with the ringing telephone, which brings the news of death. As in "Signs and Symbols," no explanation follows; the next paragraph begins with a new subject. (See *Speak, Memory*, 49, and Meyer, "Nabokov's Short Fiction," in *The Cambridge Companion to Nabokov*, 131ff. For the motif of the telephone as a memento mori in *The Gift*, see Malikova, "V. V. Nabokov and V. D. Nabokov: 'His Father's Voice,' " in *Nabokov's World*, vol. 2, 25. For the pluralistic interpretations of the story, see Wood, *The Magician's Doubts*, and Trzeciak, " 'Signs and Symbols' and Silentology," in *Nabokov at Cornell*, 58–67.)

53  See *Stories*, 599.
54  Ibid., 601, 600, 598.

> Aunt Rosa, a fussy, angular, wild-eyed old lady, who had lived in a tremulous world of bad news, bankruptcies, train accidents, cancerous growths—until the Germans put her to death, together with all the people she had worried about.[55]

Like Pnin, the couple remain silent about the unbearable past, so as to be able to exist without losing their minds. The victim of the conspiring symbols could not maintain this sanity. The mental patient is imprisoned in a world in which love drowns under waves of pain. This world is ruled by an ominous "Prince"—the nickname of the father's rich brother on whom the family is financially dependent. For no apparent reason, he is introduced in the second paragraph and shows subtly in the last that he has a hand in the fate of the mentally ill son.[56]

Under the sign of the Prince—not a bad nickname for the Demiurge—the story takes its worst turn. At the end it's no accident that the father stops his examination of the jellies at the eloquent crab apple: it is the apple of paradise gone sour, its evil parody.[57]

Scholars have also perceived a strong Gnostic undercurrent in several of Nabokov's other works. In *The Defense* it's not a confusing wallpaper pattern but the squares of a chessboard from which the hallucinating protagonist seeks to free himself. He can break out only through the escape into death. Luzhin's manager, an early diabolical character, aids his escape. In *Invitation to a Beheading* Cincinnatus is arrested for "gnostical

---

55  Ibid., 601.

56  When the father decides to bring the sick son home and have the doctor see him twice a week, he adds, "It does not matter what the Prince says." *Ex negativo*, the financier is included in the decision. (See ibid., 602.)

57  Joanna Trzeciak comes close to this interpretation when she identifies in "crab apple" the Russian "apple of paradise." It supports her and my interpretations that in the real-life prototype for the assortment (Gerber's assorted fruit jellies, identified by Brian Boyd), only one jelly is missing: the crab apple—strong evidence that it was added for a symbolic purpose. Trzeciak reads it as a reference to original sin as the root of human suffering. But in fact the crab apple is not the apple of paradise; it is its parody. The difference is best explained with a quote from G. K. Chesterton. The crab apple turns up in his work too, when he examines the shock of evil that threw Robert Louis Stevenson off course in his youth: "I do not know what it was; or what form it took; or whether it ever took any definable form at all. But somehow or other, in thought or

turpitude" and locked up in a cell to await his death.[58] He too does not escape until the moment of his execution. The novel's ending is rightfully famous. Cincinnatus's head lies on the block, the ax behind him slices through the air:

> Everything was coming apart. Everything was falling. A spinning wind was picking up and whirling: dust, rags, chips of painted wood, bits of gilded plaster, pasteboard bricks, posters; an arid gloom fleeted; and amidst the dust, and the falling things, and the flapping scenery, Cincinnatus made his way in that direction where, to judge by the voices, stood beings akin to him.[59]

Instead of dying—or, to be precise, through his death itself—the protagonist leaves behind the shabby scenery and enters an otherworldly place where the Vane sisters may be awaiting him.

In his despair by the water fountain in the park, Pnin too is on the verge of discovering the key, the solution to the universal riddle, when he is interrupted by an urgent request—we know by whom. Pnin is in the midst of thinking, "But this is the earth, and I am, curiously enough, alive, and there is something in me and in life—"[60] At this point the squirrel interrupts him. No writer—not Nabokov, at least—would have started Pnin's sentence without knowing how he would have ended it. What *is* in Pnin and in life? It seems to be something consoling after all. The Gnostic answer would be: scattered sparks of light. In a way this is also the answer given by Pnin's friend Clements. Gazing at the starry sky, he says it is "really a fluorescent corpse, and we are inside it."[61] So it is dead matter that emits light. And the colored shadows that link Victor and Pnin so closely would also have this hidden significance: darkness infused with light.

---

word or deed … he ate the apple of knowledge; and it was a crab apple." (Chesterton, *The Collected Works of G. K. Chesterton*, vol. 18, 70.)

58   *Invitation to a Beheading*, 72.

59   Ibid., 223. Malikova stresses the crucial significance of the voice in all Nabokovian memories of the beloved father. See "His Father's Voice" in *Nabokov's World*, vol. 2, 15–26.

60   *Pnin*, 58.

61   Ibid., 166.

And there's mist and light at the end of the novel: Pnin flees from an unwelcome encounter with the narrator, who has taken his job from him, and leaves Waindell. With his dog looking out the window he hurtles away, overtakes a truck, and vanishes in the distance, as the road narrows to a thread of gold in a soft mist in which "there was simply no saying what miracle might happen."[62]

That almost sounds as if Nabokov had perhaps not altered his original plan after all—even more so as Pnin's final address, 999 Todd Road, not only suggests an imminent transition into a new dimension but also contains a German word that was not unknown to Nabokov: *Tod*, or "death."[63] Does fleeing Pnin leave behind all the forest demons and demiurges? Does he break out into the true realm of light?

But we can set our minds at ease. Gnosticism and sparks of light aside: Pnin survives. In *Pale Fire* he is sitting in a Hawaiian shirt, the head of the Russian department at an American university.[64]

---

62  Ibid., 191.
63  The poem *Pale Fire* will consist of 999 lines; before the thousandth, John Shade is shot. For the symbolism of 999, see also Meyer, "Nabokov and the Spirits," 96–99.
64  See *Pale Fire*, 155, 282–83.

# 8

## SATAN & CO.

In 1942, in the same vacation house in Vermont that Pnin would visit twelve years later, Nabokov wrote his second American book, the short commissioned work *Nikolai Gogol*.[1] It's questionable how much the study conveys about Gogol, but it tells us a good deal about its author, though not because authors always write only about themselves—a half-truth that doesn't get us any further than Novalis's answer to the question "Where are we going?" ("Always home.") An author can certainly write about things other than himself, but he cannot turn off his inner sensors and smoke detectors while reading. And time and again it will happen that the outlines of his own conceptions burn so intensely in him that they are reflected back from the pages in front of him.

In the Gogol study, two things are worth noting. The first is that it begins with the leeches with which "diabolically energetic" physicians maltreat the dying Gogol, which are described as "devils … dangling from his nostrils," and ends with the "little blue flames of a humble hell" in which the continuation of *Dead Souls* burns. Between the diabolical beginning and the hellish ending a pandemonium unfolds that cannot be fully explained by Nabokov's statement that Gogol believed in the devil more seriously than he believed in God. Chichikov, the seller of souls, cannot even open his traveling chest without a circle of hell immediately opening up. Chichikov becomes the traveling salesman from Hades for the firm Satan & Co. In the first three chapters, the devil appears ten times,

---

1   Mikhail Karpovich's summer home in West Wardsboro, Vermont, was the model for "The Pines" in *Pnin*.

and the string of allusions doesn't end with the satanic soap bubbles, the "diabolically grotesque" scenes and the "reek of inferno" wafting toward the biographer.[2] There seems to be something excessive at work here, almost a compulsion under which everything takes on a satanic aspect at a mere touch.

The second noteworthy aspect of the study is related to this first one. Again with somewhat excessive intensity, Nabokov disputes any claim of realism. Nothing in Gogol has to do with the reproduction of external reality; reality itself is an inartistic concept. Gogol creates dream worlds, dreams within dreams, and secondary dream characters, recognizable in *Dead Souls* by their unusual names—a little hint for readers of *Lolita*.[3]

In light of the Gogol essay, or in its half-light, the later novel takes on a quite particular tinge. One usually reads past the devil, because he masks himself in idiom, but when Humbert complains in his journal about the inventiveness of the devil, who tempts him daily and then thwarts him, leaving him with a dull pain in the "root of [his] being," perhaps one must take this more literally. It is the same devil who ultimately realizes that he has to grant the teased man some relief if he wants to have him as a plaything for some time longer.[4] For that, various twists of fate are necessary, in which the long, hairy arm of McFate, as Humbert dubs his private devil, always plays a role.[5] First this devil sets a little fire. Humbert meets Lolita only because the McCoos' house, where he had intended to board, burned down overnight.[6] Deprived of his lodging, he wonders whether it

---

2  *Nikolai Gogol*, 1 ("diabolically energetic"), 3 ("devils ... dangling from his nostrils"), 73 ("ill-paid representative of the Devil"; "traveling salesman from Hades"; "Satan & Co."), 90 ("circle in hell"; "soap bubble blown by the devil"; "reek of inferno"), 104 ("devil's dozen"), 107 ("diabolically grotesque"), 138 ("humble hell").

3  Ibid., 42–43.

4  *Lolita*, 55–56.

5  Ibid., 56.

6  Quilty's pornographic Duk Duk Ranch also burns down in the end—which is liable to happen under the conditions of hell. The fires at the Q. (as Quilty is called) and McCoo residences are linked even more overtly in Nabokov's Russian translation. Lolita, now Mrs. Schiller, finds the burned-down ranch "so *strange*, so *strange*" and adds in Russian: "McCoo had a similar first name, his house burned down too." (See Dieter E. Zimmer's commentary to *Lolita* [Rowohlt], 639.)

wasn't the conflagration in his veins that started the fire—after all, he had spent the whole train ride indulging in lewd fantasies about the McCoos' twelve-year-old daughter. So the diabolical inferno might also be the inner fire of sexual desire; the metaphorical framework brings together both blazes.[7]

Humbert is chauffeured to Charlotte Haze's home, where he rents a room after catching a glimpse of Lolita. Shortly thereafter, he decides that marrying the mother is the best way to ensnare the daughter. Are his thoughts already wandering down tempting graveyard paths? On the wedding day, Humbert gives an interview to the Ramsdale *Journal* in which he hints that he had an affair with Charlotte thirteen years earlier. He thereby lays the groundwork for the legend that he is the twelve-year-old Lolita's biological father. The question is whether he does so only because this idea gives him an incestuous frisson and he hopes people will let a biological father get away with certain intimacies they wouldn't allow a stepfather—or whether he doesn't already anticipate the moment when he can play the grieving widower and take his little daughter under his paternal wing without the Ramsdale community becoming all too suspicious.

Suspicion of his explanations is definitely warranted. *Lolita* is an apologia from Humbert's perspective. Even though it admits much that testifies against him, it twists other things in his favor. When he assures his jurors that he did not plan to marry poor Charlotte in order to eliminate her in some "vulgar, gruesome and dangerous manner,"[8] that still leaves open the possibility of doing so in a sophisticated and safe manner. It's true that he manages to resist the first temptation, when he declines at the last moment to drown Charlotte in Hourglass Lake, though "hell screamed its counsel."[9] That he rejects this counsel saves his skin, for he is being observed from the bushes by the landscape painter Jean, who even notices

7    The McCoos' daughter is named Virginia or Ginny and is thus a surrogate Lolita in name as well, since Nabokov had originally intended to call Lolita "Virginia" and title the book *Ginny*. (See *The Annotated Lolita*, 358.)
8    *Lolita*, 70–71.
9    Ibid., 87.

that he didn't remove his wristwatch before swimming. In this case, Humbert's inner devil is more farsighted than the agent of hell.

It is this same farsightedness that will, in a devious fashion, help him achieve his goal. Humbert keeps a candid journal that he locks in his desk. Unfortunately this journal falls into the wrong hands, and as a consequence he is freed of his wife and becomes Lolita's sole guardian. But what is the status of this "unfortunately"? If Humbert had been serious about locking up his explosive notes, he would not have told Charlotte that the drawer contained old love letters; he's aware of her pathological jealousy.[10] That he knows that his so easily manipulated wife will not be able to resist this bait is revealed in an aside: though it is madness to keep this journal, Humbert tells us, his handwriting is almost illegible—"and only a loving wife could decipher my microscopic script."[11] Just as Thomas Mann's Jacob secretly knows with whom he spends his wedding night— that it's Leah and not Rachel—so too Humbert knows quite well that Charlotte will break into the drawer and discover his secret. To support this reading, Nabokov again inserts a telling adjective: Humbert writes the fatal journal in his "smallest, most satanic, hand."[12]

The satanically foreboding plan is realized: the loving wife finds the black book and deciphers the handwriting. Crossing the street in her distraught state, she is dragged to her death by a car. In her death, Satan & Co. have once again played a role. Charlotte's fatal accident is caused by a hysterical setter. Unlike the goat, the dog—in *Pnin* the protagonist's most faithful friend—is not an animal classically associated with the devil. In popular belief, however, it often appears as the companion of the person who makes a bargain with the devil.[13] Nabokov introduces it two sentences after Humbert briefly plans to travel to the islands of the Devil's

---

10  See ibid., 92.

11  Ibid., 42.

12  Ibid., 40.

13  In Goethe's *Faust*, Mephistopheles takes the form of a poodle. Goethe is drawing on a long tradition of superstition according to which the devil is often incarnated in a dog. See also Nyegaard, "Uncle Gustave's Present: The Canine Motif in *Lolita*," in *Nabokov Studies* 9 (2005), 133–55.

Triangle. En route to Charlotte's house, Humbert's driver almost runs over a "meddlesome suburban dog (one of those who lie in wait for cars)."[14] Shortly thereafter, the Haze house comes into view—the house whose mistress the dog will eliminate.

With a little help, Humbert has become the sole possessor of Lolita. But we should not deceive ourselves: she too has her subtext. Her first lover is described as a "filthy fiend,"[15] and she herself is not strictly human in nature. At least according to Humbert's definition of a "nymphet," Lolita is an "immortal daemon disguised as a female child." Making a certain movement, she resembles "the snake that may strike."[16] And Quilty, her wicked seducer—what is he if not a demon? For good reason, Humbert repeatedly calls him a devil.[17] When he finally confronts him on Grimm Road, his suspicion is confirmed. Quilty reveals his true nature:

> We fell to wrestling again. … He was naked and goatish under his robe, and I felt suffocated as he rolled over me.[18]

The goat, the traditional satanic animal, is not easy to shake off and still harder to kill. The bullets affect the poor devil as if Humbert were "injecting spurts of energy" into him.[19] Only with the greatest effort can Humbert finish off the tough sissy. And with the death of the demonic goat, the time is also ripe for that of his murderer.

Once again we may wonder where he actually makes his subsequent confession. We recall his description of his "well-heated, albeit tombal, seclusion." In addition to this euphemism, his residence in the beyond is supported by his remark that he is opposed to capital punishment "[f]or reasons that may appear more obvious than they really are."[20] The obvious assumption would be that he is threatened by it as a soon-to-be-

---

14  *Lolita*, 36.
15  Ibid., 137.
16  Ibid., 16, 139, 278.
17  Ibid., 125–27.
18  Ibid., 299.
19  Ibid., 303.
20  Ibid., 308.

condemned murderer. But if he had already preempted his execution with a heart attack, the first, self-serving motive would no longer apply, and other, less obvious ones would come into play.

And it's not always by way of euphemisms that Humbert makes insinuations about his location. At one point, he confesses quite openly that he now knows "atrocious, unbelievable, unbearable, and, I suspect, eternal horror"—how could hell be described more accurately than that?[21] Elsewhere, Nabokov dispels any remaining doubts that Humbert ultimately roasts there. In the foreword to *Despair* the author states that "there is a green lane in Paradise where Humbert is permitted to wander at dusk once a year; but Hell shall never parole Hermann."[22] Thus, 364 days a year Humbert is confined there as well—perhaps the two are cellmates.

## Dolorès Disparue

In *Nikolai Gogol* Nabokov fiercely opposed the idea that *Dead Souls* had anything to do with the reproduction of reality. Instead he saw dream worlds of various orders, which telescoped almost imperceptibly. With this insight he also provides a guiding principle for reading his most enigmatic novel. *Lolita* has a masterfully depicted realistic foreground.[23] But behind this foreground something in the stage set gradually collapses.

---

21   Ibid., 169.

22   *Despair*, xiii.

23   American everyday life around 1950, the thin-walled motels with signs that say "near churches," the cars and cigarette brands (*Camel* becomes *Drome[dary]*), the speech patterns of teenagers and the American middle class—all this is preserved forever in the Russian's novel. For all the antimimetic commandments that Nabokov preaches, we should not forget that he once called himself "half-painter, half-naturalist." (See *The Annotated Lolita*, 364.) The contradictions within his commandments are one thing; their consistency with what he does is another. For example, his principle that important spatial descriptions always have to be precise—indeed, fastidiously so—is simple, old-fashioned naturalism. One must be able to draw a map: of Ada's estate, Ardis; of Shade's or Kinbote's home; of Charlotte Haze's house. His aesthetic maxims are most beautiful and subtle when they sneak into his fiction disguised as images. The scene in *The Gift* in which an old Chinese man throws water on the reflection of flames on the walls of his dwelling says more about the relation between mimesis and mimicry than any "strong opinions." (See *The Gift*, 122.)

In addition to demons, all sorts of dream figures haunt the book. As Nabokov points out in *Nikolai Gogol*, their names alone often betray them through excessive literariness. The name Quilty has a dreamlike quality due to its confessional resonance with "guilty." A stage dialogue that never could have taken place in real life introduces Quilty to Humbert Humbert[24]—another name that can't be found in every telephone book. In the plot, the sense that something fishy's going on creeps in at the latest with Lolita's escape in the fairy-tale-like town of Elphinstone. The reader is familiar with this strange feeling from Nabokov's earlier work. In *The Gift*, Nabokov holds the scene of the father's return so artfully in suspense that the reader does not immediately realize it's a dream. Still, the novelist ultimately unmasks it as such. *Lolita* extends the earlier work to its extreme. Nothing of what happens in the last third of the book is strictly impossible; but everything warps and buckles slightly, as in a dream. There are holes and gaps in the plot, as is typical of dreams according to Nabokov's *Ulysses* interpretation.[25] Speed is distorted: Quilty dies too slowly and slips too quickly through the doors on the top floor of Pavor Manor (again, what a name!), which can be opened though they had been locked.[26] Humbert's inner and outer worlds intermingle: the buzz in his

---

24 After Charlotte's death, not much stands between Humbert and his first hotel night with Lolita, whom he picks up from Camp Q. He has devised the same sleeping-pill scheme as the eponymous enchanter in the earlier tale. Lolita is lying in bed, and as Humbert is waiting for the pills to take effect, he goes back to the hotel lobby in search of a drink. On the porch he has his first encounter with Quilty, still a stranger to him. The unreality of the dialogue between the two rivals, with its contrived Shakespeare-esque couplets, is reinforced by the arrangement of the scene. Humbert is speaking to an invisible phantom, and for no apparent reason confesses to him the death of Lolita's mother. It is the encounter with his doppelgänger or shadow, who therefore remains shrouded in darkness—or perhaps he is simply invented by Humbert later on. (See *Lolita*, 126–27.)

25 Humbert himself shares this view, when he says in summarizing his trip to Elphinstone: "after some lapses and losses common to dream sequences" (Ibid., 246). The Circe chapter in *Ulysses*, which Nabokov deciphers as a phantasmagorical dream, might be one of the models for *Lolita*'s shift into dream: "The book is itself dreaming and having visions; this chapter is merely an exaggeration, a nightmare evolution of its characters, objects and themes." (*Lectures on Literature*, 350.)

26 "I have corrected in my Russian translation a curious dream-distortion," Nabokov writes to Alfred Appel. "Q. could not be trudging from room to room since

ears turns out to be party noise; and instead of the dying Quilty, Charlotte suddenly lies beside him in the bed. The inhibitions of everyday reality fall away. As naturally as he drives on the left side of the road, Humbert tells a pushy Ramsdale acquaintance that in Camp Q. the director's son debauched all the daughters ("for shame, Mr. Humbert! The poor boy has just been killed in Korea"). After successfully fishing for information from Quilty's uncle, whom he visits in his office under the pretext of needing new dentures, he tells him that his competitor, though more expensive, is the better dentist. "It is a delicious dream feeling," he adds—a hint that the Russian version repeats for good measure.[27]

The ground under the reader's feet becomes increasingly shaky, and that seems to be Nabokov's intention. Why does Humbert state Lolita's age as 5,300 days, which means that he stopped counting on the day of her disappearance? Did he invent everything after Lolita ran away with Quilty? Is the whole last part of the novel a sort of dream?[28] Perhaps Lolita did not flee at all. Perhaps in reality she is dead.

Nabokov scattered tiny clues that support this reading too. One of the small, didactic changes he made in his translation of *Lolita* into Russian seems to point to this interpretation. A passage in the English original

---

H. H. had locked their doors, but this is okay on second thought and need not be corrected in your edition." (*Selected Letters*, 408.) Perhaps the second thought was that in dreams even locked doors are easily opened.

27    Nabokov adds to the Russian version the sentence that Humbert in his insolent behavior is availing himself of the "freedom peculiar to dreams." (See *Lolita*, 306, 290–91, and Zimmer's commentary to *Lolita* [Rowohlt], 643.)

28    This thesis of a fiction within the fiction is proposed by Dolinin (in "Nabokov's Time Doubling") and Connolly (in " 'Nature's Reality' or Humbert's 'Fancy' "). One of the arguments in its favor is a further chronological inconsistency: in the fictional foreword to the novel, John Ray Jr. gives the date of Humbert's death as November 16, 1952. At the end of the novel, however, Humbert claims to have started writing *Lolita* in captivity fifty-six days earlier. But according to his narrative, he is arrested three days after receiving Lolita's letter on September 22, 1952—that leaves only fifty-three days between his arrest on September 25 and his death on November 16. The discrepancy of three days could correspond exactly to the three days in which he finds Mrs. Schiller and murders Quilty. Here, however, one may also hazard the counter-thesis, as Boyd has done, that Nabokov this once made an oversight. See, for this and all other unresolved debates, the electronic archive of NABOKV-L.

quotes *King Lear* almost imperceptibly. After the sexual act, Humbert desperately wants forgiveness from Lolita and rocks her like a child in his "marb*le a*rms." In the Russian version, this oversubtle allusion is replaced by the overt mention of Lear, the king who cannot bear the death of his daughter Cordelia and, in his madness, speaks to her: "Cordelia, Cordelia, stay a little." Could this mean that just as Lear spoke to Cordelia in order to be with her a little longer, Humbert dreamed up a future for his dead beloved?[29]

And along with Shakespeare there is also Proust. From the beginning, allusions to *In Search of Lost Time* thread through the novel. Humbert is a Proust connoisseur and would have liked best to call the part of his story that begins with Lolita's flight "Dolorès Disparue."[30] The title is telling.

---

29   See *Lolita*, 285, and Alexander Dolinin, "*Lolita* in Russian," in *The Garland Companion to Vladimir Nabokov*, 325.

30   *Lolita,* 253. "But *you*'ve had too much Marcel"—the only reason this sentence from *Ada* could not be the epigraph of Nabokov's whole oeuvre is that one can never get enough of Marcel. (*Ada*, 169.) Nabokov's admiration for Proust was appropriately immense and grew with the decades. Early on, Nabokov transfers the problem of conscious or subconscious Proust imitation onto Sebastian Knight. (See *Sebastian Knight*, 116.) There's a long Proust pastiche in *Camera Obscura*, the predecessor to *Laughter in the Dark*. Proust's work was always the competition and the benchmark. This is evident from the catalog copy for *Speak, Memory,* which Véra wrote (anonymously) with her husband's approval and which compares him with Tolstoy and Proust. (See *Véra*, 163.) The early Nabokov, who still had to differentiate himself, opposed the self-conscious power of memory, which can flex its muscles at any time, to Proust's madeleine experience of *mémoire involontaire*. That is no longer the case in his later essay "The Art of Literature and Commonsense." There, the dissolution of time occurs in wholly Proustian fashion through involuntary memory. (See *Lectures on Literature*, 377–78.) Proust then becomes omnipresent in *Ada*, Nabokov's antiterrestrial *In Search of Lost Time*. Even Proust's sexual life is discussed in it. The transformation of an Albert into an Albertine is judged not quite successful—at least the hedonistic Van opines that Marcel's fierce jealousy of lesbian liaisons lacks psychological credibility. Nabokov is equally aware of the more peculiar inclinations of "crusty Proust who liked to decapitate rats when he did not feel like sleeping." (See *Ada*, 73 and passim.) In *Lolita* Proust's appearance as the centerpiece of Gaston's picture gallery is not his first. Nabokov introduces him in the very beginning when he has Humbert, who has already published a paper on a Proustian theme in Keats, walk near the Madeleine. (See *Lolita*, 16, 21.) In the foreword to *King, Queen, Knave*, a scallop-shaped cigarette case made Nabokov think of a similar object in *Speak, Memory*, which "quite properly" figures in the memoir, "for its shape is that of the famous *In Search of Lost Time* cake."

For in *Albertine Disparue*, the penultimate part of Proust's *In Search of Lost Time*, the following occurs: Albertine, killed in a riding accident, contacts the narrator via telegram. She is still very much alive and wants to see him and discuss marriage. Only after an agonizingly long wait do we learn that Marcel fell victim to a misreading: the telegram had been written in barely decipherable handwriting and had been falsely transmitted; in reality a different girlfriend had written to him. The beloved Albertine is and remains dead.

Also in the chapter almost titled "Dolorès Disparue," Humbert's lost love contacts him in a letter that he at first misreads. Is it possible she does so only apparently, as in Proust? During his final encounter with Lolita, now Mrs. Schiller, Humbert mentions as his destination a town with a distinctly literary name: Readsburg, where some admirers await him. It is the only place-name in the Russian translation that Nabokov did not translate as a name, but rather lexically, as Lektoburg.[31] Only there, in the fiction within the fiction, would Humbert be reunited with his vanished

---

(See *King, Queen, Knave*, ix.) Later Humbert declares that his fancy is "Proustianized." Quite properly, he makes this confession just at the moment he receives Lolita's letter, which like the telegram in *Albertine Disparue* heralds—or appears to herald—the reunion with the vanished love. (See *Lolita*, 264–66.) Scholars have not failed to recognize *Albertine Disparue* as "one of the most important (and least studied) subtexts for *Lolita* that deserves a special discussion." (See Alexander Dolinin, "*Lolita* in Russian," 330.) But it is all of Proust that is reflected in *Lolita*. Humbert's first beach love recalls the *jeunes filles en fleur*. Lolita as a captive, the betrayal of the protagonist, the flight of the beloved who is lost forever, true love as the love that is recognized too late—all this can be found in Proust, along with many other details: appeasement through gifts, the ruses of the female deceiver, the recapitulation of her sinful past after she has vanished (Humbert's search of the motels for traces and clues, Marcel's inquiries with the laundresses), and finally Lolita herself, who is as vulgar, capricious, schoolgirlish, deceitful, boyish (as need not be repeated here), and lovable as Albertine. Lolita is also modeled on Albertine in that she is ultimately a shadow and an ethereal projection. "What I had madly possessed was not she, but my own creation, another, fanciful Lolita—perhaps, more real than Lolita; overlapping, encasing her; floating between me and her, and having no will, no consciousness—indeed, no life of her own." (See *Lolita*, 62.) Here we could replace the name Lolita with Albertine without further ado and we would have one of Marcel's many reflections: when Marcel moves toward Albertine for a kiss, she flickers before his eyes into a strange, many-headed goddess.

31    See Ibid., 273, and Dolinin, "*Lolita* in Russian," 329.

love, whom he could no more bring back than Orpheus his Eurydice or Marcel his lost Albertine.

Discussing this author, one cannot escape the conditional. In his work, reality becomes volatile and ultimately vaporizes. Only its core is solid, the focus of the will, as Schopenhauer would say—or, as Humbert called it, the root of being.

# 9

## LILITH

*The corpuscles of Krause were entering the phase of frenzy. The least pressure would suffice to set all paradise loose.*

*(Lolita)*

Before Hans Castorp borrows a pencil from Madame Chauchat at the carnival festivities—a pencil that he will later return to her in her room—Settembrini warns him: "Look closer now, my lad! ... 'Tis Lilith." The name means nothing to Castorp. Nor does he have Goethe's *Faust* in mind as he unwittingly quotes it in his question: "Who?" Delighted, his mentor echoes Mephisto's reply: "The first wife Adam had. You'd best beware ..." Chauchat's admirer is taken aback—he had no idea that Adam was married twice. Settembrini informs him that according to Hebrew tradition he was. Lilith became a wraith who haunts young men by night; her beautiful hair makes her particularly dangerous.

"Herr Urian sits atop them all," the unsuccessful admonisher quotes resignedly once again from Goethe's "Walpurgis Night" shortly thereafter.[1] As a nocturnal ghost and demon Lilith is also associated with this Herr Urian. According to Jewish lore, God created Lilith as a wife for Adam, but Lilith refused to submit to God's command to live under Adam's dominion. The reason for her insubordination: the clay out of which God created her had been contaminated by the saliva of the outcast

---

1 Mann, *The Magic Mountain*, 389–93. In the edition cited, "Herr Urian" is replaced by the devilish American folk character "Old Scratch," and the line reads: "Old Scratch himself atop them all."

Samael. It is not only in the Weber opera *Der Freischütz* that Samael, the demon of the Talmud and the Aramaic "poison of God," is a name for the devil.

After quarreling with Adam, Lilith moves out of Paradise into the desert; from that point on she gives birth to demons. Adam complains of loneliness, whereupon God creates Lilith's successor, Eve, out of Adam's rib. Unlike Eve, Lilith remains immortal, because she did not eat from the Tree of Knowledge. Some suspect that she herself inhabited the snake that convinced Eve to eat the apple. She becomes more and more demonic with the years. Once a man has been seduced by Lilith, he never escapes.

Nabokov, too, was aware of all this when he wrote his poem "Lilith" in 1928:

> I died. The sycamores and shutters
> along the dusty street were teased
> by torrid Aeolus.
> I walked,
> and fauns walked, and in every faun
> god Pan I seemed to recognize:
> Good. I must be in Paradise.
> Shielding her face and to the sparkling sun
> showing a russet armpit, in a doorway
> there stood a naked little girl.
> She had a water lily in her curls
> and was as graceful as a woman. Tenderly
> her nipples bloomed, and I recalled
> the springtime of my life on earth,
> when through the alders on the river brink
> so very closely I could watch
> the miller's youngest daughter as she stepped
> out of the water, and she was all golden,
> with a wet fleece between her legs.
> And now, still wearing the same dress coat
> that I had on when killed last night,
> with a rake's predatory twinkle,
> toward my Lilith I advanced.
> She turned upon me a green eye
> over her shoulder, and my clothes

were set on fire and in a trice
dispersed like ashes.
               In the room behind
one glimpsed a shaggy Greek divan,
on a small table wine, pomegranates,
and some lewd frescoes covering the wall.
With two cold fingers childishly
she took me by my emberhead:
"now come along with me," she said.
Without inducement, without effort,
Just with the slowness of pert glee,
like wings she gradually opened
her pretty knees in front of me.
And how enticing, and how merry,
her upturned face! And with a wild
lunge of my loins I penetrated
into an unforgotten child.
Snake within snake, vessel in vessel,
smooth-fitting part, I moved in her,
through the ascending itch forefeeling
unutterable pleasure stir.
But suddenly she lightly flinched,
retreated, drew her legs together,
and grasped a veil and twisted it
around herself up to the hips,
and full of strength, at half the distance
to rapture, I was left with nothing.
I hurtled forward. A strange wind
caused me to stagger. "Let me in!"
I shouted, noticing with horror
that I again stood outside in the dust
and that obscenely bleating youngsters
were staring at my pommeled lust.
"Let me come in!" And the goat-hoofed,
copper-curled crowd increased. "Oh, let me in,"
I pleaded, "otherwise I shall go mad!"
The door stayed silent, and for all to see
writhing with agony I spilled my seed
and knew abruptly that I was in Hell.[2]

_____

2 *Poems and Problems*, 51–55.

This scene expresses something elemental. Its author is only twenty-eight when he writes it, but *Lolita* is already shimmering on the horizon. Humbert, that novel will inform us, was "perfectly capable of intercourse with Eve, but it was Lilith he longed for."[3] The poem not only anticipates Humbert's longings and nightmares; "Lilith" also prefigures the uncomfortable seclusion in which he is writing. The lyric "I" is a dead man who finds himself in hell. At first he had thought it was paradise. Clearly life does not end with death and there is a danger of confusion between paradise and hell. The paradise of unrestrained pleasure with the seductress is unmasked as the hell of coitus interruptus and shame. Fully erect, the protagonist is exposed to a gaping crowd. This anxious vision winds its way perceptibly through Nabokov's work. Adam Krug, too, falls victim to a Lilith:

> [T]he widower's heavy sensuality seeks a pathetic outlet in Mariette, but as he avidly clasps the haunches of the chance nymph he is about to enjoy, a deafening din at the door breaks the throbbing rhythm forever.[4]

In a flash the skies of paradise turn the "color of hell-flames," as Humbert puts it. His greatest wish is to "sort out the portion of hell and the portion of heaven" in his nymphet love; but it is the one wish that remains unfulfillable.[5] The moment he senses the secret unity and describes the hell that awaits him is also the moment of elemental exposure: Humbert is

---

3   *Lolita*, 20. The poem "Lilith" also prefigures Van Veen's games with Ada, which are observed by their little sister. In an intricate way it is a quite comical scene: the lovers tie Lucette to a tree with a skipping rope to steal a few precious minutes for a tryst. When they return, the sister is fumbling with her rope as if she were on the verge of freeing herself. Later they learn that the spy was actually trying to tie herself up again. "Good lord," Van comments, when he learns of this, "that explains the angle of the soap!" (In the bathtub Lucette had later reenacted with the soap what she'd seen. See *Ada*, 143, 144, 152.) In *Pale Fire* it is Kinbote's slim-haunched friend Fleur who inspires a sculptor's *Lilith Calling Back Adam*; a call that only a homosexual Adam could resist. See *Pale Fire*, 108.
4   See Nabokov's foreword to *Bend Sinister*, xvii. Here Lilith is christened Mariette. More on this character on 128, n. 44.
5   *Lolita,* 166, 135. When Dolores makes phone calls, then naturally it is to "Paradise, Wash., Hell Canyon." (Ibid., 296.)

driving with Lolita on a high mountain pass. At a secluded spot below the tree line he spreads a lap robe. Venus comes and goes. He is lying naked beside sobbing Lolita and laughing happily. The "eternal horror" he knows *now*, at the time of his writing, is

> still but a dot of blackness in the blue of my bliss; and so we lay, when with one of those jolts that have ended by knocking my poor heart out of its groove, I met the unblinking dark eyes of two strange and beautiful children, faunlet and nymphet, whom their identical flat dark hair and bloodless cheeks proclaimed siblings if not twins.[6]

As in "Lilith," it is children who catch the satyr in his nakedness: twins who were already present at Humbert's almost-murder of Charlotte in Hourglass Lake and who, dark-haired and pale, are also waiting on the davenport after the murder of Quilty.[7]

*Lolita*'s predecessor, *The Enchanter*, takes the theme a step further and makes the victim herself the witness. Humbert's forerunner stalks a rollerskating girl on a playground and courts her mother. After the mother's death, he takes the unsuspecting daughter to a hotel. He doesn't want to do her any harm—the child shall go on sleeping as he snuggles up to her, as Marcel did with Albertine.[8] But just as his life is about to be

---

6   Ibid., 168–69.

7   Mabel and Marion are riding their bicycles through the woods by the lake and could have witnessed from concealment the murder Humbert ultimately refrains from committing. As telltale stones come rolling from under the pines, Charlotte does not suspect the hobby painter Jean who is hidden there, but rather the "disgusting prying kids." After Quilty's murder, two dark-haired, pale sisters are demurely sitting side by side on a davenport. (Ibid., 84, 88, 304.)

8   The literary prototype of the finale to *The Enchanter* is the "la regarder dormir" passage from Proust's novel. Marcel snuggles up to the sleeping Albertine and embarks, in an extended sea-and-wave metaphor, "upon the tide of [her] sleep." He is gently rocked by the regular motion of her breathing. Sometimes it affords him a pleasure that is "less pure": he allows his leg "to dangle against hers, like an oar which one trails in the water, imparting to it now and again a gentle oscillation. ... The sound of her breathing, which had grown louder, might have given the illusion of the panting of sexual pleasure, and when mine was at its climax, I could kiss her without having interrupted her sleep." Earlier in the passage, we read: "Carriages went rattling past in the street, but her brow remained as smooth and untroubled ..." The sleeping girl is wearing a kimono. In an echo of the title of the volume, she is called a "charming

reduced to the "simplicity of paradise" and he is on the verge of "sense-lessly discharging molten wax," she awakes and starts to scream in shock.[9] As in "Lilith," paradise turns out to be hell. Caught in the act, the enchanter attempts to escape from this hell by throwing himself under the wheels of a thundering truck.

At the heart of the Lilith poem, *The Enchanter*, and *Lolita*—at the heart of Nabokov's whole metaphysical–erotic cosmos—lies the merging of opposites into a single point. Sexual desire is heaven and hell—and shame reigns over both. It grows not only with the intensity of the longing, but also with its deviance. Sirin's Lilith reaches "childishly" for her excited admirer. Once a man has fallen under her spell, he never escapes.

## Poisoned Apples

*When ... he really let himself go and pottered happily on the brink of his private abyss, he became the greatest artist that Russia has yet produced.*

(Nabokov, *Nikolai Gogol*)

Everything erotic in *Lolita* is stunning—young Humbert on the Riviera with Annabel, whose "quivering mouth" seems "distorted by the acridity of some mysterious potion"; Lolita eating an apple on his "tense, tortured, surreptitiously laboring lap" and the "glowing tingle" of "absolute secu-rity" that comes over his senses when he is "suspended on the brink of that voluptuous abyss"; Lolita's anklet with which he deceives Charlotte; the first night with the nymphet in the hotel, with the surprising about-face that it is beauty who seduces the beast ...[10]

---

captive." (*In Search of Lost Time*, vol. V, 87–88, 85.) And here is Nabokov in compar-ison: the sleeping girl is wearing a robe (because she couldn't find her nightgown). We read about the "flow and ebb" of this robe in an appropriation of the sea-and-wave motif. The trucks howling past, which presage the enchanter's suicide, cannot disturb her sleep; she just gives a brief moan and glides back into her previous torpor. The enchanter lies down "to the left of the captive." He snuggles up to her legs and achieves his less pure pleasure. The scene with Lolita bringing Humbert to orgasm without knowing it (or does she know it?) while eating an apple is likewise a variation on this night of the enchanter. (See *The Enchanter*, 69–74.)

9  Ibid., 74.
10  See *Lolita*, 14, 60, 81, 128–34.

Strictly speaking, *Lolita* was only half-misunderstood. It is, of course, not a pornographic novel, but it renders burning sexual desire in language that none of Nabokov's notoriously obscene contemporaries—neither D. H. Lawrence nor Henry Miller—could equal. The audience might have had insufficient appreciation of the artistry of the prose, but it was not completely misguided to perceive the novel's bestial dimension, which is reflected in Humbert's famous concluding sentence: "I am thinking of aurochs and angels"—that is, of the earliest, poignant art of cave painting, but also of the animal instinct, which is resolved with the angelic and ethereal only in the immortality of art.[11]

Part of this audience drew a specific conclusion from its half-misunderstanding: whoever could imagine a full-grown man assaulting a thirteen-year-old girl three times a day (as is specified in the Russian translation) must himself be a monster. Nabokov was confronted with this judgment in attenuated form even from his friends, particularly in the prudish United States. His declaration in *Strong Opinions* that one day a reappraiser would come and recognize him as a rigid moralist "kicking sin, cuffing stupidity, ridiculing the vulgar and cruel—and assigning sovereign power to tenderness, talent, and pride" is directed against those critics.[12] Today this reappraisal would be unnecessary. No one will deny that Nabokov kicked sin and cuffed stupidity—or vice versa if one prefers.

Were those critics, however, completely on the wrong track when they drew a line from what was depicted to the depicter? Undoubtedly, they did so with much oversimplification and a disregard for all philological principles and taboos. As if he anticipated them, Nabokov expressed his preemptive derision for these philistines early on: in *Nikolai Gogol* he scoffs at "the morbid inclination we have to derive satisfaction from the

---

11   Ibid., 309. The novel's ending is already anticipated in a program text for the cabaret *Karussel* from 1922, which relates winged seraphim to prehistoric animal paintings. Nabokov rightly likens his early works to butterfly pupae, in which the wings appear in miniature shortly before the final transformation. (See *Eigensinnige Ansichten*, 194, 180.)

12   *Strong Opinions*, 193.

fact (generally false and always irrelevant) that a work of art is traceable to a 'true story.' Is it because we begin to respect ourselves more when we learn that the writer, just like ourselves, was not clever enough to make up a story himself?"[13] And so why, to be consistent with this argument, don't we leave aside altogether the experience that underlies or precedes the fiction? The emulsion of what is read, experienced, and imagined cannot be dissolved—certainly not when it comes to the great authors. Indeed, this very indissolubility is one of the marks of their greatness.

But Nabokov himself isn't entirely consistent in this regard. It's understandable that, after *Lolita*, he felt compelled to post a "Beware of Dog" sign—even if a forest of warning signs such as Nabokov planted first had to wake the sleeping dogs. But when the day of John Shade's murder falls on Vladimir Nabokoff's birthday or when "Clare Bishop" is code for Véra Slonim—to give two examples remote from *Lolita*—how are we to understand these cryptographic references if we leave aside the life? And that is to say nothing of the artificiality and sterility of such an exclusion, an exercise in kicking and cuffing common sense.

The case of *Lolita* might in fact be akin to one of the chess problems that Nabokov composed for pleasure. In one of these compositions, he devised a position that seems to demand an ultrasophisticated solution. Only after hours of enjoyable detours does the expert discover the actually quite simple solution—a move that the amateur would have found in five minutes.

With *Lolita* something similar might be going on. Nabokov has insisted that if he had any obsessions, he would be careful not to reveal them in novelistic form.[14] Still, the ordinary reader would suspect that a

---

13  *Nikolai Gogol*, 40. Nabokov puts an entirely different sentiment into the mouth of the narrator of "Spring in Fialta": "Personally," he confesses, "I never could understand the good of thinking up books, of penning things that had not really happened in some way or other … were I a writer, I should allow only my heart to have imagination, and for the rest rely upon memory, that long-drawn sunset shadow of one's personal truth." (*Stories*, 420.) That's more naïve than Nabokov would have put it, of course, and the idea of the heart's imagination leaves all sorts of doors open. Still, the final image is quite close to the author's distinctive tone.

14  See *Eigensinnige Ansichten*, 183.

book like this was surely written because the author wanted to get something off his chest. There are two or three points that support this suspicion.

When it comes to *Lolita* Nabokov disregards his sacred aesthetic laws. In all other instances, he reliably flew into a rage whenever someone imputed symbols to him. But *Lolita* is supposedly not about sex with young girls—anything but that. The red herrings he employs are striking: the most famous is the story of the ape in the Jardin des Plantes who drew the bars of its cage, thus inspiring Nabokov's novel. But how does one get from an ape to an irresistible young girl, if one didn't already have the latter in mind?

The true story of *Lolita* is that of decades of cautiously feeling his way to the center and inner core. First Nabokov makes women into girls only metaphorically. Then he gradually lets the veil of camouflage fall, until he suddenly tears it away completely in *The Enchanter*.

Lolita has bashful predecessors from the beginning.[15] Nabokov is twenty-four when he puts the first nymphet in the story "Revenge." Feeling "light as a young girl," the delicate, small, flat-chested woman slips into the bedroom, where a skeleton awaits her.[16] Two years later a fourteen-year-old girl in a low-cut party dress appears in "A Nursery Tale" in the company of an elderly poet, whom Nabokov himself later recognized as a forerunner of Humbert. There's something peculiar about this girl's face:

> odd was the flitting glance of her much too shiny eyes, and if she were not just a little girl—the old man's granddaughter, no doubt—one might suspect that her lips were touched up with rouge. She walked swinging her hips very, very slightly, her legs moved closer together.[17]

---

15  See also the thorough enumeration by Zimmer in *Lolita* (Rowohlt), 532–37.
16  See *Stories*, 69, 72.
17  Ibid., 170, 648. In *Pale Fire*, the character Fleur, who is compared with Lilith, has the same swinging gait, a way of walking that "Arab girls were taught in special schools by special Parisian panders who were afterwards strangled." (*Pale Fire*, 108.)

And the protagonist can no more resist her than can all his successors. The "Nursery Tale" nymphet is also already very much Lolita in that she is offered to him by none other than the devil.[18]

Nor does it take long for her to make her presence felt in his novels. In *King, Queen, Knave* we already catch a fleeting glimpse of a schoolgirl for whom the protagonist longed ages ago.[19] The next child-woman leads the unfortunate Albinus to his ruin in *Laughter in the Dark*. In the Russian version, *Camera Obscura*, she is also only officially a mature woman—with her "slim girlish figure" and the "childish lines of her body" she seems like a young girl.[20] The veil has slid down even further with Emmie, the mysterious, lascivious young girl in *Invitation to a Beheading* who likes to sit on the condemned man's lap.

The first plot outline of *Lolita* already appears in *The Gift*. "Ah, if only I had a tick or two," sighs Fyodor's landlord—and this sigh is anything but innocent—"what a novel I'd whip off!"

> Imagine this kind of thing: an old dog—but still in his prime, fiery, thirsting for happiness—gets to know a widow, and she has a daughter, still quite a little girl—you know what I mean—when nothing is formed yet but already she has a way of walking that drives you out of your mind—A slip of a girl, very fair, pale, with blue under the eyes—and of course she doesn't even look at the old goat. What to do? Well, not long thinking, he ups and marries the widow. Okay. They settle down the three of them. Here you can go on indefinitely—the temptation, the eternal torment, the itch, the mad hopes.[21]

---

18  The devil, who appears here as a masculine woman, offers the protagonist, Erwin, the unique opportunity to select a harem for himself; all he has to do is desire a woman, and she'll be his. The one condition: the total of the concubines must be an odd number. Erwin bungles the job, because he inadvertently chooses the same woman twice. But the nameless Lolita is actually to blame. In a September 1966 letter to Field, Nabokov explained: "The thing that gives the story its chief charm is that he would have had his harem if he had not added the nymphet (No. 12) to his list, since the odd number, eleven, would not have been changed to an even number by the addition of the last, already selected girl (No.1)." (Boyd, *The Russian Years,* 259.)

19  *King, Queen, Knave,* 202.

20  *Laughter in the Dark,* 58, 92.

21  *The Gift,* 186. The would-be novelist does not get the idea for this Dostoyevskian tale out of nowhere; it is his own story. He has made advances to young Zina; his

And here Nabokov did go on. Finally, after the failed attempt of *The Enchanter*,[22] he managed to complete successfully the monster of a book in Ithaca, New York.

Is it not safe to assume, the layperson would ask again, that so deep-rooted a theme has sprung from the heart? What is most striking is not even that Lolita has forerunners—it's that she has successors. After the novel, the coveted women remain child-women. Lilith does not relinquish her hold on Nabokov. Indeed, she preoccupies him up to his last novel.

## Lolita's Double: The Original of Laura

There is, there was, only one girl in my life, an object of terror and tenderness ... I say "girl" and not woman, not wife or wench.

(*The Original of Laura*)

How old is Ada when Van tastes her apple? A tender twelve—which is easy to miss, because the incest diverts attention from it. In his old age Van's father takes pleasure in ten-year-olds. So too in Nabokov's last published novels, *Transparent Things* and *Look at the Harlequins!*, it is girls on the verge of pubescence who are coveted. When the protagonist of the ghost novel, Hugh Person, leafs through his beloved's photo album, his eyes are inexorably drawn to the prepubescent girl's spread legs and the "middle line just distinguishable from the less vertical grass-blade next to it," and he shuts the book with a guilty wince when he's interrupted in this viewing.[23]

---

marriage is a failure; perhaps, like Humbert later, he married the mother only to get close to the daughter.

22    In the afterword to *Lolita* Nabokov recalls this failed attempt: "I read the story one blue-papered wartime night to a group of friends—Mark Aldanov, two social revolutionaries, and a woman doctor; but I was not pleased with the thing and destroyed it sometime after moving to America in 1940." (*Lolita*, 312.) In the last point his memory had deceived him; the manuscript turned up in 1959 and was published in 1986, nine years after Nabokov's death, in translation by his son, Dmitri, under the title chosen by the author, *The Enchanter*.

23    See *Transparent Things*, 41.

And finally there's the *opus posthumum*, *The Original of Laura*—the manuscript of the last, unfinished novel, long steeped in legend: 138 index cards that Nabokov in his illness told his family to destroy and that Dmitri, after decades of hesitation, presented to the public in the fall of 2009. A hesitation that was only too understandable: Nabokov's last will actually left no room for interpretation. The writer was prudish in matters of unfinished manuscripts and didn't want to give people a peek into his workshop. On the other hand: What about his famous predecessors from Virgil to Kafka, whose testamentary instructions were disobeyed, much to the joy of posterity? And hadn't *Lolita* itself almost fallen victim to an auto-da-fé that was then fortunately averted? Perhaps in the case of *Laura*, too, Nabokov would have reconsidered his decision, which might have been made in a similar moment of weakness. And yet: Could one disregard his express wish, in a sense wresting from his hands something unfinished to which he clung?

Difficult questions. Ultimately, Véra, who died in 1991, and his only son and heir could not bring themselves to comply with Vladimir's demand and consign *TOOL* (his acronym for his last work) to the flames—though Dmitri threatened to do so for a while and seemed already to have wielded the match.[24] Even if he ultimately did not carry

---

24   The question first seemed to become highly charged in the fall of 2005. Dmitri Nabokov, seventy-one years old at the time, had implied in an e-mail that he would execute his father's will and burn the *Laura* manuscript, which was located in a Swiss bank vault. The announcement circulated in the international press and led to an article by Ron Rosenbaum in the *New York Observer* beseeching Nabokov's son to spare the manuscript and entrust it to a library. On November 25, Dmitri sounded an ambiguous "all-clear" signal in the Russian *Kommersant*: he had neither carried out nor even announced the manuscript's incineration; he hadn't yet made the decision. In the two subsequent years, Dmitri didn't seem any closer to a decision, but he periodically made threats. Even the indefatigable Ron Rosenbaum, though he sympathized with Dmitri's "Hamlet-like dilemma," implored the guardian of *TOOL* in the online magazine *Slate* to lay his cards on the table. The time had come to decide one way or the other: "The suspense is killing me." (See Ron Rosenbaum, "Dmitri's Choice," in *Slate*, January 16, 2008.) Finally, in April 2008, Dmitri unexpectedly declared his intention to publish the manuscript. The reasons he has invoked since are legion and somewhat conflicting. If nothing else, the argument that his smiling father made in an imaginary spectral conversation probably convinced him: "Well, why don't you mix the useful with the

out this threat, the main reason he gave for it is telling. It was less out of consideration for his father's last will than concern about "Lolitology."[25]

Like his long indecision, this concern, too, is understandable. If *Ada* already bore marks of a late work with relaxed self-censorship, in *Laura* the last remaining veils and inhibitions fall away. More sorrowful and privately eccentric than the great love story, the brilliance of which it fails to achieve, the fragment is disappointing from an artistic perspective—all the more so as the hints Dmitri had dropped about the new aesthetic shore his father had supposedly reached had been so rhapsodic as to make the mouths of Nabokovians water.[26] Still, *The Original of Laura* powerfully reveals an author who is grimly or solemnly determined to deal with his life's themes one last time—which means retelling for the last time the story of the "one girl."

The sick old man's sexual life is "virtually over,"[27] and now only death awaits him. He resolves to wangle from it his last pleasure through a

---

pleasurable? That is, say or do what you like but why not make some money on the damn thing?" (Quoted in Ron Rosenbaum, "The Fate of Nabokov's *Laura*," in *Slate*, April 25, 2008.) The *Playboy* advance alone for the right to serialize *Laura* was supposedly the highest in the magazine's history. One would rather not imagine the long faces when Laura finally lays bare her scant charms.

25  Lolitology: publications dealing with his father's most famous work that Dmitri felt to be undignified and impious. One of these disgraceful writings presented the discovery of a German novella that shared a theme and title with *Lolita*, but had been written by a Nazi. (See Maar, *The Two Lolitas*.) Due to this last fact, the mere question of whether Nabokov, who had lived in Berlin for fifteen years, could have taken notice of the German *Lolita* author, Heinz von Lichberg, was tantamount to slander. On the Internet forum NABOKV-L, a Russian Nabokovian alluded indignantly to his family's wartime fate. Another participant in the forum drew the conclusion with which Dmitri himself seemed to be flirting at the time: *The Original of Laura* should be burned along with the "pulp story by von Wotsisname." Only the purity of the flames would protect *Laura* from the dirty hands of the critics.

26  Dmitri called the manuscript "the most concentrated distillation of [my father's] creativity." *The Original of Laura* "would have been a brilliant, original, and potentially totally radical book, in the literary sense very different from the rest of his oeuvre." (Quoted in Ron Rosenbaum, "Dmitri's Choice," in *Slate*, January 16, 2008.)

27  *The Original of Laura*, [101]. In this respect, Philip Wild is distinct from the shah whose widow bequeathes a fountain to Flora's university. (See also 126, n. 32.) "The potentate had been potent till the absurd age of eighty." (Ibid., [51].)

special trick. Half of *The Original of Laura*[28] deals with the strange suicide technique of the unhappily married neurologist Dr. Philip Wild, who attempts to think himself into nonexistence from the toes upward through meditation.[29] "Suicide made a pleasure"—that's the plan.[30] In the hypno-trance that the excessively corpulent protagonist strives to attain, sheer force of will is to triumph over the infirm body: "The process of dying by auto-dissolution afforded the greatest ecstasy known to man."[31]

If one wanted to describe the thought experiment Nabokov performs here in mythical terms, one could say: Thanatos has defeated Eros, and now the loser has one last, desperate chance—to beguile the victor. The book's subtitle is *Dying is Fun*, and half of the manuscript is devoted to the attempt to imbue death with erotic pleasure.

---

28   Half of the novel is, to be precise, a sixth, for about two-thirds are missing, according to Dieter E. Zimmer's reckoning in his afterword to the German translation. (See *Das Modell von Laura*, 307.)

29   Dr. Wild hates his toes and feet (which, as Dmitri acknowledges for once, had also tormented his father at the time of *Laura*'s composition). Detail is mostly welcome, but the expansive elaborations on old age in *Laura*—involving indigestion, flatulence, constipation, diarrhea, foot odor, and prostate tumors—have a grim, masochistic note, less reminiscent of Nabokov, for whom life was bread and honey, than of late Tolstoy and his above-mentioned *tartine de merde*. The insatiable girls, on the other hand, game for every "quickie," as they often are in old men's fantasies, are reminiscent of late Arno Schmidt and pre- or postpotent resentment. (*The Original of Laura*, [16].) There's also resentment in Nabokov's almost compulsive sideswipes against—who else? "Dr. Freud, a madman," and Saint-John Perse, alias "St. Leger d'Eric-Perse" (ibid., [45])—Nobel Prize, 1960—as well as against his contemporaries, "stunning mediocrities" with their "most execrable writing": "Malraux, Mauriac, Maurois, Michaux, Michima, Montherland and Morand" (ibid., [48], [49])—a list of authors who, inci-dentally, not only bear names starting with the letter *M,* but are also, for the most part, scarcely attracted to women. Thomas Mann undoubtedly escaped the list only by dying in the nick of time.

30   Ibid., [64].

31   Ibid., [82], [86]. The process is one of "self-obliteration conducted by an effort of the will. Pleasure, bordering on almost unendurable ecstasy, comes from feeling the will working at a new task: an act of destruction which develops paradoxically an element of creativeness in the totally new application of totally free will." (Ibid. [107].) This somewhat Buddhistic experiment in practical metaphysics is also linguistically far less compelling than the dark metaphysical cosmos into which Nabokov previously drew us. Dying is *not* fun.

The other, livelier half of *The Original of Laura* is about the painful memory of the time when Thanatos was still a shadow and Eros reigned.[32] Regarding the nature of this Eros, few doubts remain. On all fictional levels of this mutilayered novel, including in the book within the book—the bestseller *My Laura*, for which a character named Flora is the model—Eros has the face of a young girl.[33]

Flora, the titular original of Laura, is as promiscuous and lustful as Ada, and betrays her husband, Philip Wild, whenever she can. The true original of Flora, however, is not Ada, but Lolita. Flora is twelve when she's fondled by her mother's lover—a Mr. Hubert H. Hubert, who since his departure from Ramsdale has lost his *m* but is otherwise very much his old self. As in *Lolita*, Hubert Hubert abuses the mother's trust to make advances to the daughter. As in *Lolita*, he prowls around her, mesmerizing and cornering her.[34] As in *Lolita*, there is a love of his youth who dies at the age of twelve and fixates the man's longing forever on *fillettes*: Hubert

---

32   Though Thanatos already cast its shadow on Eros early on: Flora met her later husband Philip Wild at the moment her mother collapsed dead during a ceremony on Flora's campus. The ceremony was the unveiling of a fountain, which did not go off without problems. "The fountain took quite a time to get correctly erected after an initial series of unevenly spaced spasms." (Ibid., [51].) It's not only this fountain—famous since *Pale Fire* for its liability to be misprinted—that shows how Eros, in the shadow of Thanatos, creeps into the cells of the language. Another example, which once again displays the old Nabokovian brilliance, is the miniature chess set on which Flora—"she knew the moves"—plays with Mr. Hubert Hubert: though "the pin-sized pawns penetrated easily" into the little holes in the squares, the "slightly larger noblemen had to be forced in with an enervating joggle." (Ibid., [33].)

33   The *Laura* novel is sent to Dr. Wild by a painter named Rawitsch, a rejected admirer of his wife, Flora. Years earlier Rawitsch made an oil painting of Flora. Wild only reluctantly opens the book, but then discovers it to be a "maddening masterpiece." (Ibid., [110], [111].) Of course, the true book within the book is not *My Laura*, but *Lolita*, which that characterization quite accurately describes and on which Nabokov meditates in his twilight years. Flora, the woman with the breasts of a twelve-year-old girl, not only inspires the artist, but also plays a formative role in his composition: "Her exquisite bone structure immediately slipped into a novel—became in fact the secret structure of that novel ..." (Ibid., [8].)

34   Humbert's predecessor, the enchanter of the posthumously published story of the same name, makes an explicit reappearance as well: "He looked now like a not too successful conjuror paid to tell fairytales to a sleepy child at bedtime, but he sat a little too close." (Ibid., [32].)

Hubert tells Flora about his daughter, who was the same age as she when he lost her in an accident. And Philip Wild falls in love with Flora only because she resembles an early, deceased love: not Annabel Leigh, but Aurora Lee.[35]

There is and was only one woman in Wild's life, and she was not a woman, but a girl. It is the magic of this early age that he rediscovers in Flora and that binds him to her. Even if she's no longer twelve, he turns her back into a nymphet by subtraction—"the cup-sized breasts of that twenty-four year old [sic] impatient beauty seemed a dozen years younger than she."[36] Time and again when he praises her physical beauty he lets slip the age he truly desires. Her shoulder blades are "the mobile omoplates of a child being tubbed."[37] And when he describes the only position in which he can still sleep with Flora in his obesity, he chooses the following image: "holding her in front of him like a child being given a sleigh ride down a short slope by a kind stranger."[38]

There was certainly nothing like this in *Lolita*. Much that was only faintly hinted at becomes drastic and explicit in *The Original of Laura*. The little surprise that Dr. Wild discovers during his exploration of Aurora's genitals has already been mentioned.[39] It's not the only allusion to homosexual acts in Nabokov's literary testament. As if we were in Thomas Mann's late *Felix Krull*, the protagonist falls for the androgynous allure of a brother and sister. His dream of Aurora leaves him with the strong impression of her "little bottom, so smooth, so moonlit, a replica, in fact, of her twin brother's charms." At this point there's a parenthetical aside that jars

---

35  In the manners of his characters' deaths, too, Nabokov becomes increasingly extreme. Young Aurora "was to be axed and chopped up at seventeen by an idiot lover, all glasses and beard." (Ibid., [103].) In the book within the book, Laura dies the "craziest death in the world," which is not explained further. (Ibid., [114].) Flora, her model, lives at least long enough to have the paperback in her lap; by reading it, she can learn the circumstances of her fictitious death. Dr. Wild dies, in spite of all his meditation, of a banal heart attack. (Ibid., [94].)

36  Ibid., [8].

37  Ibid., [10].

38  Ibid., [99], [100].

39  See 33, n. 23.

us abruptly out of the Platonic, moonlit sphere: "sampled rather brutally on my last night at boarding school."[40]

Nor is this an isolated allusion to brutal practices in boarding schools and colleges. In addition to an old don watching boys bathing (a peeping don, as it were),[41] there's a minor character named Eric who confesses to a particular sexual predilection due to the "unforgettable impact of my romps with schoolmates of different, but erotically identical, sexes."[42]

Different sex, same Eros. Boy and girl can coalesce, as in Wild's licentious dream. There's only one thing that never fails to cause aversion: mature womanhood. What Eric and Dr. Wild convey is of course the characters' point of view. It's likewise a character's point of view when Fyodor in *The Gift* expresses the "painful disgust" that women outside of a particular type evoke in him.[43] But in one passage it's not a fictional character, but the author himself who can scarcely conceal a certain disgust. In his commentary to *Eugene Onegin*, Nabokov describes a picture in which Tatiana in an open nightdress bares her full breast. Slightly repulsed, he calls it a "fat breast."[44]

---

40   *The Original of Laura*, [104].

41   Ibid., [11].

42   Ibid., [118]. The details of Eric's predilection: "I much preferred—madly preferred—finishing off at my ease against the softest part of her thigh." Whether the young Nabokov himself came into contact with such romps in Cambridge is a question at least worth considering; certainly he must have heard about them.

43   See *The Gift*, 329.

44   See *Eugene Onegin*, vol. II, 178. It's not for no reason that Field asks whether Nabokov actually liked women and answers: "In his fiction, at least, by and large not." (*Life and Art*, 163.) In fact, this is only half true, for in Nabokov's work there are two classes of women: that of the good, selfless, loving spouses like Luzhin's wife, Zina Mertz in *The Gift*, Clare Bishop in *Sebastian Knight*, Olga Krug in *Bend Sinister*, and Sybil Shade in *Pale Fire*; and the larger group of bitches, the first of which appears in *King, Queen, Knave*. The most monstrous member of this group, Mariette in *Bend Sinister*, certainly provides strong evidence for Field's thesis. Mariette marks the low point in Nabokov's work. The young, pretty nymph who serves the toad Paduk and is ordered to seduce the poor widower Krug is a female character portrayed so hatefully in every single detail that one almost wants to defect to the Freudians out of protest. Mariette is erotically alluring, vain, dumb, vulgar, deceitful, nymphomaniacal, and cruel to children; she delivers Krug's son, David, to his tormentors and serenely puts on makeup as he cries desperately for his father. After the evil woman has been punished

LILITH

## Vicious Circle with Palm Tree

There is yet another reason to assume that in *Lolita* Nabokov follows the motto of the Elizabethan poet Sir Philip Sidney: " 'Fool!' said my Muse to me, 'look in thy heart, and write.' " It is something elusive, a question of tone. To gain a sense of this tone, we might imagine how we tend to react to a reproach that is not quite true, but also not entirely false—that, strictly speaking, may even be largely accurate. "That's not *exactly* right," we say in such cases, and in our defense we become verbose, elaborate, digressive, and at times vehement and are certainly not in command of ourselves.

It is this very tone that we occasionally hear from Nabokov. As soon as he wishes to explain something subtle and urgent that lies close to his heart and to defend it against an obvious charge, his voice takes on an unmistakable intonation. To call this voice strained and artificial is to escape into metaphor, but it is hard to describe it any other way. Indeed, it is metaphors that characterize these passages: they are labored, far-fetched; they hyperventilate, as it were, and yet have the deeply personal tone of truth, which manifests itself precisely in the overstatement. In life, we reply, "That's not *exactly* right," and start to ramble on. In the following two examples, Nabokov gives this reaction literary expression.

In *Sebastian Knight* the charge is that Sebastian left his wife for sexual reasons. To refute this the narrator ranges far afield. The very word *sex* with its hissing "ks" at the end he rejects in its rasping vulgarity. Besides, "physical love is but another way of saying the same thing." And finally he quotes from Sebastian's story "The Back of the Moon":

> The breaking of a wave cannot explain the whole sea, from its moon to its serpent; but a pool in the cup of a rock and the diamond-rippled road to Cathay are both water.[45]

Ah, yes, we understand—and in life would draw the conclusion: he probably left his wife in part for sexual reasons.

---

by Paduk for the mix-up of children to which David falls victim, we see her in a prison cell as she "gently bleeds, staked and torn by the lust of forty soldiers," as Nabokov tells us with, alas, unmistakable satisfaction. (See the foreword to *Bend Sinister*, xiv.)

45   *Sebastian Knight*, 105.

The second example: in the fifth chapter of *The Gift* Fyodor is walking through the pinewoods in Grunewald. When a young girl comes toward him, he feels the "impact of a hopeless desire," for she has that "fascination, both special and vague," which he finds in many girls. Shortly thereafter, his eyes—along with those of three other voyeurs—burn a hole in the bathing suit of a young "nymph."[46] Fyodor rejects the obvious conclusion that he is fixated on a particular female type:

> Oh trite demon of cheap thrills, do not tempt me with the catchword "my type." Not that, not that, but something beyond that. Definition is always finite, but I keep straining for the faraway; I search beyond the barricades (of words, of senses, of the world) for infinity, where all, all the lines meet.[47]

On this side of the barricades, in the trite, finite world, where parallel lines do not intersect, one would conclude: no question, he's stuck on a type.

After these samples, we come to the justification that the narrator of *The Enchanter* gives for his fixation on nymphets—or less a justification than a rumination in which he seeks clarity about his deviance. "How can I come to terms with myself?" the novel begins:

> What is it then? Sickness, criminality? And is it compatible with conscience and shame, with squeamishness and fear, with self-control and sensitivity? For I cannot even consider the thought of causing pain or provoking unforgettable revulsion.

One more reason for the protagonist of Sebastian Knight's last novel to regret on his deathbed not having spoken to that schoolgirl, who instead of revulsion offered him shameless eyes. "Nonsense," the enchanter, having just revealed himself to be a moralist, goes on:

> I'm no ravisher. I'm a pickpocket, not a burglar. Although, perhaps, on a circular island, with my little female Friday ...[48] (it would not be a question

---

46   *The Gift*, 329, 335–36. The word *nymph*, still without diminutive, reveals the sunbather as a proto-Lolita.

47   Ibid., 329.

48   So there is a higher logic to the fact that *Lolita* would be brought out by the publisher of *The Sexual Life of Robinson Crusoe*.

of mere safety, but a license to grow savage—or is the circle a vicious one, with a palm tree at its center?).

Gradually he slips into the forced defensive tone that is still ringing in our ears:

> Knowing, rationally, that the Euphrates apricot is harmful only in canned form; that sin is inseparable from civic custom; that all hygienes have their hyenas; knowing, moreover, that this selfsame rationality is not averse to vulgarizing that to which it is otherwise denied access ... I now discard all that and ascend to a higher plane.
>
> What if the way to true bliss is indeed through a still delicate membrane, before it has had time to harden, become overgrown, lose the fragrance and the shimmer through which one penetrates to the throbbing star of that bliss? Even within these limitations I proceed with a refined selectivity; I'm not attracted to every schoolgirl that comes along, far from it.

Not every girl can be a nymphet, as we learn from Humbert, who declares this category a third, demonic sex. The impact of a hopeless desire strikes the enchanter, like Fyodor, only in the presence of a very specific type. How this desire can arise from loving feelings, whether as a "natural complement" or a "demonic contradiction," gives him a further quandary to ponder:

> [O]ften I have tried to catch myself in the transition from one kind of tenderness to the other, from the simple to the special, and would very much like to know whether they are mutually exclusive, whether they must, after all, be assigned to different genera, or whether one is a rare flowering of the other on the Walpurgis Night of my murky soul; for, if they are two separate entities, then there must be two separate kinds of beauty, and the aesthetic sense, invited to dinner, sits down with a crash between two chairs (the fate of any dualism). On the other hand, the return journey, from the special to the simple, I find somewhat more comprehensible: the former is subtracted, as it were, at the moment it is quenched, and that would seem to indicate that the sum of sensations is indeed homogeneous, if in fact the rules of arithmetic are applicable here.[49]

---

49  *The Enchanter*, 3–6.

Does one hear how seriously Nabokov takes this, and how this seriousness is reflected precisely in the characteristic style: monologic, ruminating, as if straining for a solution rather than striving for readability? And let us not forget that he is writing this passage in extreme distress at the low point of his life, amid the battle noise of the German troops and in the awareness that he might be composing his last work.

A decade later, Humbert picks up the thread of ruminations about coming to terms with nymphet desires. He merely brings into sharper focus what is already adumbrated with Fyodor (who in the posthumous second volume of *The Gift* engages the same young prostitute with whom Humbert later finds pleasure).[50] Humbert, though, is clearer on the origins of his proclivity. He traces it back to an arrested experience in his early youth. His beach love, Annabel, with whom he had his first taste of pleasure—only to be caught again by voyeurs—is snatched from him.[51] Annabel dies four months after their separation. As a result of this shock, his desire becomes fixed forever. Annabel is the "initial fateful elf" on whom he models all his subsequent girls. Lolita, too, is only a revenant of the original nymph. With his first love, Humbert declares, "the poison was in the wound, and the wound remained ever open."[52]

In interviews Nabokov spoke out against interpreters who were reminded by Humbert's Riviera romance of the episode in *Speak, Memory* in which the author describes his first love for Colette.[53] The innocent love of the ten-year-olds on the beach is in fact distinct from the erotic enchantment that young Humbert experiences. This is not the case, however, with Nabokov's recollections of his relationship with Tamara, whom he immortalized in his first novel as Mashen'ka. She was the first erotic love and fulfillment of his fifteen years. Whether she was also the one who trickled sweet poison into a wound that remained open, the

---

50  Boyd, *The Russian Years*, 517.

51  When Humbert is on the point of possessing Annabel on the beach, two "bearded bathers" come out of the sea "with exclamations of ribald encouragement." There is something so strange about this scene that one is inclined to attach the adjective *primal* to it. (See *Lolita*, 13.)

52  Ibid., 18.

53  See *Strong Opinions*, 24.

memoir does not reveal. The Tamara motif in *Invitation to a Beheading* could be interpreted in this light.

But to come back to that distinctive tone: Why is Humbert's voice, so unlike that of the enchanter, not strained and forced, but in command in all registers? A tricky question. The reason could be that Nabokov covertly makes him more evil. The earlier victims of nympholepsy were just that: victims, for whom one had sympathy in spite of all revulsion. Was not the pseudo-pasha of "A Nursery Tale," who is tempted by the devil and gets hung up on a fourteen-year-old girl, ultimately a poor worm? Was not the enchanter one too, when he threw himself under the wheels in shame? Humbert is many things, but a poor worm he is not. What Fyodor still expressed in tones of lyrical justification, Humbert turns into a predatory onslaught. And herein lies the breakthrough that Nabokov achieves with *Lolita*.

He artfully staggers the perspectives for the first, second, and third glance. At first glance Humbert is a lecher who robs a poor girl of her childhood. At second glance he remains a lecher, but at the same time has some appealing qualities, much wit and sarcastic candor. Humbert is actually not an unsympathetic character—at least not until the reader notices the details that Nabokov intersperses for the third glance.

Not only does the novelist have Humbert commit unforgivable errors in the classification of insects.[54] He also makes him unnecessarily cruel. Humbert twists the wrist of his first wife, Valeria, when she disagrees with him—indeed, the very wrist that is especially sensitive due to a biking accident. Valeria's equally sensitive legs he resolves to "[hurt] very horribly" when he finds out about her lover. He refers to her later death in childbirth as his "little revenge."[55] He is also meaner to Lolita than he has to be. He purchases her only listlessly granted favors with little "monetary bribes" that he takes back from her after the act.[56] Twice he pries open her hand afterward to reclaim his sinful sum. He also postcoitally retracts

---

54   Humbert confuses little moths of the genus *Pronuba* with white flies and mistakes a swarm of hawk moths for hummingbirds. (*The Annotated Lolita*, 390.)

55   See *Lolita*, 83, 29, 30.

56   Ibid., 148, 183–85.

promises he made to her beforehand. Child abuse is bad enough, but one should keep one's promises! Nabokov's hatred for him is unmistakable.

Finally, however, there is the fourth glance. Even a monster can reform. It is disputed whether Humbert's famous self-accusation—on the precipice of the valley from which the sounds of children's voices rise, a concord from which Lolita's voice is absent—should be understood as his final attempt to ingratiate himself with the reader through feigned remorse in a sort of *qui s'accuse, s'excuse*.[57] But the fact that Humbert, in parting from a pregnant Lolita whose nymphet charms have faded, bursts into the desperate tears of true love cannot be denied by even the sternest reader. Humbert comes too late to love, as one can come too late to one's senses. Herein lies the tragic dimension of which Nabokov does not want to deprive him. The "pentapod monster" is condemned to hell, but not entirely: once a year he is permitted to wander on the green lane, because in the end he loves Lolita.[58]

All the author's sympathy is reserved for her. How often does Nabokov speak of poor Lolita, the heartrending little girl, the child sacrificed on the altar of the motel?[59] He himself—who must distance himself from Humbert—had as a child kept his father waiting because his uncle had held him too long on his lap. Both beauty and the beast, it seems, are invested with aspects of the self—and perhaps herein lies the novel's secret.

The novelist describes its tragic finale in elevated terms: after the emotional tempest of sensual passion, Humbert in the end experiences human and divine love.[60] It is only through divine love that the Lilith

---

57  Michael Wood, for example, is skeptical: Wood simply can't buy Humbert's remorse, calling it "too good to be true." (See *The Magician's Doubts*, 139–40.) Boyd is equally mistrustful of the passage. (See *The American Years*, 252–54.)

58  See *Lolita*, 284.

59  See, for example, the November 1959 interview with Anne Guérin in *L'Express*, in *Eigensinnige Ansichten*, 42.

60  October 1959 interview published in *Art, Lettres, Spectacles*. The interview was conducted by Alain Robbe-Grillet, one of the few contemporary authors of whom Nabokov had a high opinion and the only one he compared with Proust. It is one of the early, unpolished interviews in which he had not yet established the ritual of having

demon is finally exorcized. Sensual love is always infused with darkness. There is never sexuality in Nabokov's work without demonic shadows and guilt. In *Ada*, Van curses nature "for having planted a gnarled tree bursting with vile sap within a man's crotch."[61] The tree is known to cause trouble—with the snake coiled around it, it brings about the great exile from Paradise. At the same time, the spasm of the sexual act, as we learn in *Ada*, is the only moment when reality loses the quotes it wears like claws: it is the gateway to the true world.[62]

Thus this world must be profoundly suspect and dubious at its heart. This doubt harbored by Nabokov as a secret Gnostic, coupled with a quivering passion for the fragrance and shimmer of the world, lends his work the tension that it will continue to impart to us readers for a long time.

## The Chinese Master

*But my inward fantasies and representations have reduced and consumed my outward life; and this only because I represented them.*

(*Jean Paul*)

When he was on the point of burning the dangerous manuscript, he was stopped by the thought that "the ghost of the destroyed book would haunt my files for the rest of my life."[63] But would it have confined itself to his files? What would have prevented Lolita from haunting his life too? If ghosts are not pressed between the covers of a book, they are hard to contain—and perhaps that is precisely why they must be pressed between

---

questions submitted to him in advance so he could write prepared answers, and it is quite funny at points. Robbe-Grillet asks about the national peculiarities of reactions to *Lolita* and Nabokov describes them to him: in India and Turkey no one could see any reason to make so much fuss about things that are so normal and natural. In Japan they put a voluptuous, blond woman on the cover—"Lolita Monroe," as it were. Nabokov had been particularly surprised by Sweden, where the book had been as flat as a louse: they had apparently left in only the slightly risqué scenes and had cut everything else. (See *Eigensinnige Ansichten*, 35–36.)

61  *Ada*, 479.
62  Ibid., 220.
63  *Lolita*, Afterword, 312.

the covers. Perhaps something is exorcized in literature that threatens to take root in life. Perhaps that is in fact the goal: to rid life of its demons through fiction.

It would be a healthy, cleansing, soothing transformation. But there is a flipside: Nabokov experienced the deleterious effects literature can have on life. When he depicted someone in his work, the real person withered; the Swiss governess of his childhood, whom he immortalized in "Mademoiselle O," lived on only meagerly in his memory after her transformation into fiction. *The Original of Laura*, too, had been intended to deal with the way the neurotic author destroys his model through the portrait. This betrayal of the man by the storyteller could trouble Nabokov: "One hates oneself for leaving a pet with a neighbor and never returning for it."[64]

And over the years Nabokov left behind a veritable zoo. But that's the relatively harmless side of the matter. Nabokov expressed his opposition to the method, which he nonetheless practiced, of using other people as models. But what about the author himself? Even when he drew from others, he derived most of his material from the richness of his permeated self. So what are we to make then of the pet for which no one returns?

The subject of the suffering writer is a cliché, which was enough to make it anathema to Nabokov in his later years. Only rarely did he drop a hint, as he did once in a conversation with Andrew Field: "My life, I wouldn't call it boring ... but it has been so ... it has been centered so much on literature, on writing ..."[65] He puts another hint into the mouth of the protagonist of *The Gift*. Fyodor has long since realized "that he was incapable of giving his entire soul to anyone." Only in a dream, in the longed-for encounter with his father, does his "icy heart" melt like that of the fairy-tale boy in the Snow Queen's palace.[66] The only moments akin to this scene are the descriptions of ecstasy in *Speak, Memory*, when the

---

64    *Strong Opinions*, 143. "The man in me revolts against the fictionist," Nabokov writes in "Mademoiselle O." (*Stories*, 480.) Andrew Field reports in a similar vein: "[H]e felt that using these scenes in his fiction had deprived his memories of their life." (*Life and Art*, 47.)

65    Field, *Life and Art*, 367.

66    *The Gift*, 178, 355. A similar theme is sounded at the end of Nabokov's early drama *The Pole*.

writer burdened with the gift elevates his love for his wife and son to a cosmic level, when he draws radii from the "nucleus of a personal matter" to "monstrously remote points of the universe":

> When that slow-motion, silent explosion of love takes place in me, unfolding its melting fringes and overwhelming me with the sense of something much vaster, much more enduring and powerful than the accumulation of matter or energy in any imaginable cosmos, then my mind cannot but pinch itself to see if it is really awake.[67]

The compulsion to survey the universe in all directions in order to measure his feeling against it—that, too, is Nabokov's art. That, too, lies behind his depictions of failures and aberrations, the whole spectrum of the monstrous against which the "nucleus of a personal matter" must assert itself. That he was capable of this emphasis kept him from becoming the narcissist whose grimaces he conjures everywhere as a self-protective magic. He was certainly capable of despair, as the dark side of his work shows—a side that seems to negate itself with the last word on the last index card of *The Original of Laura*: "obliterate."[68] His despondency wasn't like that of Thomas Mann, who in the depression of his later years so often quoted the line from Shakespeare's *Tempest*, "And my ending is despair." But Nabokov was familiar with the gradual absorption of the self into fiction.

It already began in his childhood bedroom, where there hung a picture of a forest into which he longed to climb and disappear.[69] This old Chinese motif surfaces in his early story "La Veneziana" and winds through his work from that point on. As the art merges more and more with the self, the self dissolves in the art.

---

67  *Speak, Memory*, 296–97.
68  *The Original of Laura*, [138]. The manuscript ends on an almost Beckettian note with a string of annihilating verbs: "efface expunge erase delete rub out wipe out obliterate." It's haunting how, in the last word Nabokov wrote, literature exists only in negation.
69  *Speak, Memory*, 86. In the opening pages of the novel *Glory* there is also a picture of a forest hanging over Martin's childhood bed—a forest in which Martin will ultimately disappear without a trace. (See *Glory*, 4.)

In the old Chinese tale, a painter has grown old and lonely over his work. And when he has finally completed it, he invites his remaining friends to see it. His guests have formed their judgments and are about to tell them to the artist, but they no longer find him among them. He has vanished. Finally they discover him in his own painting, where he follows the path up the hill to the house, opens the little gate, and turns around one last time. Waving, he takes leave of his faithful companions and closes the gate firmly behind him.

So, too, does Nabokov close the gate behind him, leaving his interpreters in their confusion. Their quarrels grow ever fainter in the midst of his art, a garden of forking paths on which one strays with so much joy.

# BIBLIOGRAPHY

## Cited Works by Vladimir Nabokov

*Ada, or Ardor: A Family Chronicle*, New York: Vintage International, 1990.

*Bend Sinister*, New York: Vintage International, 1990.

*The Defense*, New York: Vintage International, 1990.

*Despair*, New York: Vintage International, 1989.

*The Enchanter*, New York: Vintage International, 1991.

*Eugene Onegin: A Novel in Verse, Volume I: Introduction and Translation*, Princeton, N.J.: Princeton University Press, 1975.

*Eugene Onegin: A Novel in Verse, Volume II: Commentary and Index.* Princeton, N.J.: Princeton University Press, 1975.

*The Eye*, New York: Vintage International, 1990.

*The Gift*, New York: Vintage International, 1991.

*Glory*, New York: Vintage International, 1991.

*Invitation to a Beheading*, New York: Vintage International, 1989.

*King, Queen, Knave*, New York: Vintage International, 1989.

*Laughter in the Dark*, New York: Vintage International, 1989.

*Lectures on Literature*, San Diego, New York, and London: Harcourt, 1980.

*Lolita*, New York: Vintage International, 1997.

*The Annotated Lolita*, New York: Vintage Books, 1991.

*Look at the Harlequins!* New York: Vintage International, 1990.

*Mary*, New York: Vintage International, 1989.

*Nikolai Gogol*, New York: New Directions, 1971.

*The Original of Laura: A Novel in Fragments*, New York: Knopf, 2009.

*Pale Fire*, New York: Vintage International, 1989.

*Pnin*, New York: Vintage International, 1989.

*Poems and Problems*, New York and Toronto: McGraw–Hill International, 1970.

*The Real Life of Sebastian Knight*, New York: New Directions, 1959.

*Selected Letters, 1940–1977*, San Diego, New York, and London: Harcourt, 1989.

*Speak, Memory*, New York: Vintage International, 1989.

*The Stories of Vladimir Nabokov*, New York: Vintage International, 1997.

*Strong Opinions*, New York: Vintage International, 1990.

*Transparent Things*, New York: Vintage International, 1989.


## Sources

Bang, Herman, "Gedanken zum Sexualitätsproblem," in *Forum Homosexualität und Literatur* 10 (1990), with an introduction by Heinrich Detering.

*Berliner Tageblatt*, no. 119, March 29, 1922.

Cheever, John, *The Journals of John Cheever*, New York: Knopf, 1991.

Chesterton, Gilbert Keith, *The Collected Works of G. K. Chesterton*, vol. 18, San Francisco: Ignatius Press, 1991.

Dunne, J. W., *An Experiment with Time*, London: Faber & Faber, 1958.

——, *The New Immortality*, London: Faber & Faber, 1938.

——, *The Serial Universe*, London: Faber & Faber, 1938.

Forster, Leonard (ed.), *The Penguin Book of German Verse*, Harmondsworth, U.K.: Penguin Books, 1959.

Hirschfeld, Magnus (ed.), *Jahrbuch für sexuelle Zwischenstufen unter besonderer Berücksichtigung der Homosexualität*, Leipzig: Verlag von Max Spohr, 1899–1903.

Kafka, Franz, *The Blue Octavo Notebooks*, ed. Max Brod, trans. Ernst Kaiser and Eithne Wilkins, Cambridge, U.K.: Exact Change, 1991.

Karlinsky, Simon (ed.), *Dear Bunny, Dear Volodya: The Nabokov–Wilson Letters, 1940–1971, Revised and Expanded Edition*, Berkeley, Los Angeles, and London: University of California Press, 1979.

Mann, Thomas, *Death in Venice and Other Stories*, trans. David Luke, New York: Bantam Books, 1988.

——, *Diaries, 1918–1939*, ed. Hermann Kesten, trans. Richard and Clara Winston, New York: Harry N. Abrams, 1982.

——, *Doctor Faustus*, trans. John E. Woods, New York: Vintage International, 1997.

——, *The Magic Mountain*, trans. John E. Woods, New York: Everyman's Libary, 1995.

Proust, Marcel, *In Search of Lost Time, Volume V: The Captive & The Fugitive*, trans. C. K. Scott Moncrieff and Terence Kilmartin, rev. D. J. Enright, New York: Modern Library, 1992.

Schopenhauer, Arthur, *Der handschriftliche Nachlaß in fünf Bänden,* ed. Arthur Hübscher, Munich: DTV, 1985.

——, *The World as Will and Representation, Volume I,* trans. E. F. J. Payne, New York: Dover Publications, 1966.

——, *The World as Will and Representation, Volume II,* trans. E. F. J. Payne, New York: Dover Publications, 1966.

## Secondary Literature

Alexandrov, Vladimir E., *Nabokov's Otherworld,* Princeton, N.J.: Princeton University Press, 1991.

——, *The Garland Companion to Vladimir Nabokov* (Garland Reference Library of the Humanities vol. 1474), New York: Routledge, 1995.

Appel, Alfred, Jr., "Backgrounds of *Lolita,*" in *TriQuarterly* 17 (1970): "*For Vladimir Nabokov on His Seventieth Birthday,*" ed. Charles Newman, 17–40.

——, "Lolita: The Springboard of Parody," in *Nabokov: The Man and His Work,* ed. L. S. Dembo, 106–43.

Barabtarlo, Gennady, *The Nabokov Research Newsletter* 9 (1982).

——, *Phantom of Fact: A Guide to Nabokov's Pnin,* Ann Arbor: Ardis, 1989.

Boyd, Brian, *Nabokov's Pale Fire: The Magic of Artistic Discovery,* Princeton, N.J.: Princeton University Press, 1999.

——, *Vladimir Nabokov: The American Years,* Princeton, N.J.: Princeton University Press, 1991.

——, *Vladimir Nabokov: The Russian Years,* Princeton, N.J.: Princeton University Press, 1990.

Collins, Emily, "Nabokov's Lolita and Andersen's *The Little Mermaid,*" in *Nabokov Studies* 9 (2005), 77–100.

Connolly, Julian W. (ed.), *The Cambridge Companion to Nabokov,* New York and Cambridge, U.K.: Cambridge University Press, 2005.

——, "'Nature's Reality' or Humbert's 'Fancy,'" in *Nabokov Studies* 2 (1995), 41–61.

——, "*Pnin*: The Wonder of Recurrence and Transformation," in *Nabokov's Fifth Arc,* ed. J. E. Rivers and Charles Nicol, 195–210.

Davydov, Sergej, "*Invitation to a Beheading,*" in *The Garland Companion to Vladimir Nabokov,* ed. Vladimir E. Alexandrov, 188–203.

Dembo, L. S. (ed.), *Nabokov: The Man and His Work,* Madison, Milwaukee, and London: University of Wisconsin Press, 1967.

Diment, Galya, *Pniniad: Vladimir Nabokov and Marc Szeftel,* Seattle and London: University of Washington Press, 1997.

# BIBLIOGRAPHY

Dolinin, Alexander, "*Lolita* in Russian," in *The Garland Companion to Vladimir Nabokov*, ed. Vladimir E. Alexandrov, 321–30.

——, "Nabokov's Time Doubling: From *The Gift* to *Lolita*," in *Nabokov Studies* 2 (1995), 3–40.

Evans, Walter, "The Conjuror in 'The Potato Elf,'" in *Nabokov's Fifth Arc*, ed. J. E. Rivers and Charles Nicol, 75–81.

Ferger, George, "Who's Who in the Sublimelight: 'Suave John Ray' and Lolita's 'Secret Points,'" in *Nabokov Studies* 8 (2004), 137–98.

Field, Andrew, *VN: The Life and Art of Vladimir Nabokov*, New York: Crown Publishers, 1986.

Foster, John Burt, Jr., "Nabokov and Proust," in *The Garland Companion to Vladimir Nabokov*, ed. Vladimir E. Alexandrov, 472–81.

Grayson, Jane, Arnold McMillin, and Priscilla Meyer (eds.), *Nabokov's World, Volume 1: The Shape of Nabokov's World*, Hampshire, U.K., and New York: Palgrave, 2002.

——, *Nabokov's World, Volume 2: Reading Nabokov*, Hampshire, U.K., and New York: Palgrave, 2002.

Grishakova, Marina, "V. Nabokov's *Bend Sinister*: A Social Message or an Experiment with Time?" in *Sign Systems Studies* 2, Tartu, Estonia: Tartu University Press, 2000, 242–63.

Grossman, Lev, "The Gay Nabokov," in *Salon*, May 17, 2000, http://www.salon.com/books/feature/2000/05/17/nabokov/

Grossmith, Robert, "Spiralizing the Circle: The Gnostic Subtext in Nabokov's *Invitation to a Beheading*," in *Essays in Poetics* (September 1987), 51–74.

Johnson, D. Barton, "Vladimir Nabokov and Walter de la Mare's 'Otherworld,'" in *Nabokov's World, Volume 1*, ed. Jane Grayson et al., 71–87.

——, *Worlds in Regression: Some Novels of Vladimir Nabokov*, Ann Arbor: Ardis, 1985.

Johnson, D. Barton, and Brian Boyd, "Prologue: The Otherworld," in *Nabokov's World, Volume 1*, 19–25.

Kelly, Catriona, "Nabokov, Snobizm and Selfhood in *Pnin*," in *Nabokov's World, Volume 2*, ed. Jane Grayson et al., 117–40.

Kuzmanovich, Zoran, "Strong Opinions and Nerve Points: Nabokov's Life and Art," in *The Cambridge Companion to Nabokov*, ed. Julian W. Connolly, 11–30.

——, "Suffer the Little Children," in *Nabokov at Cornell*, ed. Gavriel Shapiro, 49–57.

——, (ed.), *Nabokov Studies, Volume 1–9*, Davidson, N.C.: Davidson College.

Langen, Timothy, "The Ins and Outs of *Invitation to a Beheading*," in *Nabokov Studies* 8 (2004), 59–70.

Maar, Michael, "Everlasting Men," in *Die falsche Madeleine*, Frankfurt am Main: Suhrkamp Verlag, 1999, 114–28.

——, *Geister und Kunst: Neuigkeiten aus dem Zauberberg*, Munich: Hanser Verlag, 1995.

——, *The Two Lolitas*, trans. Perry Anderson, London and New York: Verso, 2005.

Malikova, Maria, "V. V. Nabokov and V. D. Nabokov: 'His Father's Voice,'" in *Nabokov's World, Volume 2*, ed. Jane Grayson et al., 15–26.

Meyer, Priscilla, "Dolorous Haze, Hazel Shade: Nabokov and the Spirits," in *Nabokov's World, Volume 2*, ed. Jane Grayson et al., 88–103.

——, "Nabokov's Short Fiction," in *The Cambridge Companion to Nabokov*, ed. Julian W. Connolly, 119–34.

Morgan, Joanne, *Solving Nabokov's Lolita Riddle*, Sydney: Cosynch Press, 2005.

Nyegaard, Ole, "Uncle Gustave's Present: The Canine Motif in *Lolita*," in *Nabokov Studies* 9 (2005), 133–55.

Parker, Stephen Jan (ed.), *The Nabokovian* 30 (Slavic Languages & Literatures), University of Kansas, Spring 1993.

Pellérdi, Márta, "Nabokov's *The Real Life of Sebastian Knight* or, What You Will," in *Kodolányi Füzetek* 5, Working Papers, ed. Kiszely Zoltán, Székesfehérvár, Hungary: Kodolányi János University College, 1999.

Pifer, Ellen, *Vladimir Nabokov's* Lolita: *A Casebook*, Oxford, U.K.: Oxford University Press, 2003.

Proffer, Carl R., *A Book of Things About Vladimir Nabokov*, Ann Arbor: Ardis, 1974.

Proffer, Carl R., and Ellendea Proffer (eds.), *Russian Literature Triquarterly*, Ann Arbor: Ardis, 1991.

Quennell, Peter (ed.), *Vladimir Nabokov, His Life, His Work, His World: A Tribute*, London: Weidenfeld and Nicolson, 1979.

Quispel, Gilles, "Gnosticism from its Origins to the Middle Ages," in *The Encyclopedia of Religion, Volume 5*, ed. Mircea Eliade, New York: Macmillan, 1987, 1995.

Rampton, David, "Nabokov and Chesterton," in *Nabokov Studies* 8 (2004), ed. Zoran Kuzmanovich, 43–57.

Rivers, J. E., "Proust, Nabokov, and *Ada*," in *Critical Essays on Vladimir Nabokov*, ed. Phyllis A. Roth, Boston: G. K. Hall, 1984, 134–56.

# BIBLIOGRAPHY

Rivers, J. E., and Charles Nicol (eds.), *Nabokov's Fifth Arc: Nabokov and Others on His Life's Work*, Austin: University of Texas Press, 1982.

Rosenbaum, Ron, "Dmitri's Choice," in *Slate*, Jan. 16, 2008, http://www.slate.com/id/2181859/pagenum/all/

——, "The Fate of Nabokov's *Laura*," in *Slate*, April 25, 2008, http://www.slate.com/id/2190065/pagenum/all/

Roth, Phyllis A. (ed.), *Critical Essays on Vladimir Nabokov*, Boston: G. K. Hall, 1984.

Rowe, W. W., *Nabokov's Spectral Dimension*, Ann Arbor: Ardis, 1980.

Schiff, Stacy, *Véra: Mrs. Vladimir Nabokov*, New York: Modern Library, 1999.

Shapiro, Gavriel (ed.), *Nabokov at Cornell*, Ithaca, N.Y.: Cornell University Press, 2003.

Trzeciak, Joanna, "*Signs and Symbols* and Silentology," in *Nabokov at Cornell*, ed. Gavriel Shapiro, 58–67.

Wood, Michael, *The Magician's Doubts: Nabokov and the Risks of Fiction*, Princeton, N.J.: Princeton University Press, 1994.

——, "Nabokov's Late Fiction," in *The Cambridge Companion to Nabokov*, ed. Julian W. Connolly, 200–212.

Zimmer, Dieter E., *A Guide to Nabokov's Butterflies and Moths*, Hamburg: self-published, 1996.

——, *Nabokovs Berlin*, Berlin: Nicolaische Verlagsbuchhandlung, 2001.

——, *Wirbelsturm Lolita*, Reinbek: Rowohlt Verlag, 2008.


For all citations from the German editions of *Lolita, Pnin*, and *Sebastian Knight,* as well as *Eigensinnige Ansichten*, the German collection of interviews, see Dieter E. Zimmer (ed.), *Vladimir Nabokov: Gesammelte Werke*, Reinbek: Rowohlt Verlag.


For the German translation of *The Original of Laura*, see Dieter E. Zimmer (ed.), *Das Modell für Laura (Sterben macht Spaß). Romanfragment auf 138 Karteikarten*, trans. Dieter E. Zimmer and Ludger Tolksdorf, Reinbek: Rowohlt Verlag, 2009.

# INDEX

# INDEX